A QUESTION OF VALUE

A QUESTION OF VALUE

STORIES FROM THE LIFE
OF AN AUCTIONEER

Robert Brunk

THE UNIVERSITY OF NORTH CAROLINA PRESS

Chapel Hill

Designed by Jamison Cockerham
Set in Arno and Adelar
by codeMantra

Cover photos of fork and coins courtesy of Brunk Auctions.

Manufactured in the United States of America

LIBRARY OF CONGRESS CATALOGING-IN-PUBLICATION DATA
Names: Brunk, Robert S., author.
Title: A question of value : stories from the life of an auctioneer / Robert Brunk.
Description: Chapel Hill : The University of North Carolina Press, 2024.
Identifiers: LCCN 2023034112 | ISBN 9781469678092 (paperback ; alk. paper) |
ISBN 9781469678108 (ebook)
Subjects: LCSH: Brunk, Robert S. | Auctioneers—United States—Biography. |
Mennonites—United States—Biography. | Consumers—United States—Psychology. |
United States—Social life and customs—20th century. |
United States—Social life and customs—21st century.
Classification: LCC N8604.B76 A3 2024 | DDC 381/.17092 [B]—dc23/eng/20230804
LC record available at https://lccn.loc.gov/2023034112

publication supported by a grant from Figure Foundation

To Jeremy

CONTENTS

AUTHOR'S NOTE

In the interest of privacy, names, places, and dates have been altered in several essays.

Every effort has been made to report dialogue accurately and to make it consistent with the context: person, time, and place.

"Rifle" was first published as "A Mennonite Soldier" in *Under the Sun*, 2016.

"Shingle" was first published as "A Samuel Beckett Song" in *Michigan Quarterly Review*, Fall 2013.

"Log," "Piano," "Forest," and "Doorway" were first published in different forms under the title "Selling Everything" in the *Iowa Review*, Spring 2014.

"Video" was first published as "A Conceptual Work of Art" in *Alaska Quarterly Review*, Spring 2018.

A
QUESTION
OF
VALUE

DOORWAY

There were hundreds, maybe thousands, of cats: porcelain, silver, wood, glass, bronze, fabric, and wire cats, paintings and prints of cats sleeping, sitting, stalking, playing. Some were well made, others flimsy tourist souvenirs. It was 1986, and I found myself in a three-story brick house in Georgia, several years into my work as an auctioneer, in a spacious area known to the family as the cat room.

The daughter of the woman who had passed away encouraged me to look around. I opened one of eight doors to storage cabinets on a wall and saw a dozen snow globe music boxes. All made in China, stacked in a row in their original unopened boxes, they featured smiling cats sitting in snow. I opened more doors and found dozens of Christmas ornaments, small plastic dolls, and ceramic figurines, all new in unopened boxes, and all with a cat or kitten in some predictable pose.

Another client, a single woman in her late seventies, lived in a large mountain home with three spacious walk-in closets, each with rows of expensive dresses, coats, sweaters, and fashionable designer ensembles, most with their original price tags. Racks and drawers overflowed with hundreds of purses, gloves, sweaters, hats, belts, shoes, and pricey costume jewelry; most of it appeared to be new.

I have been in a home in which the owners had collected and stored in a walk-in safe forty-five sets of sterling silver flatware. In another estate, a four-room house was required to store and display the doll collection.

The essays in this book begin in the late 1970s, when I attended my first auctions; include stories after I became a licensed auctioneer in 1983; and extend to my retirement from the business I founded, Brunk Auctions, in 2013. In those thirty-odd years, I lived in Asheville, North Carolina, and was witness to the remarkable variety of objects to which people were attracted. At its peak, roughly 1980–2010, this collecting in the Asheville area was fed by twenty antique shops and fifteen auctioneers specializing in antiques and collectibles. But that hustling ecosystem of local commerce has largely vanished, replaced by the temptations of the Internet.

A career as an auctioneer might seem strange for someone raised, like me, in the Mennonite church. Implicit in Mennonite beliefs and traditions is an unspoken rejection of mindless consumerism. In making decisions about our life work, we were encouraged not to ask, "What do I want?" but rather, "What needs to be done?" In this Mennonite culture, clothes, shoes, tools, appliances, food, vehicles, furniture, buildings, lumber, stones, land, and waterways were repaired, adapted, and reused. Relationships were rarely discarded; divorce was uncommon.

I had an uncle who only bought socks of the same brand and color, dark blue. If one sock was ever lost or worn out beyond repair, he found a matching sock and never needed to buy another pair or throw one sock away. It wasn't merely a matter of recycling: it was about owning far fewer things to begin with. Creativity might find expression in a colorful and finely stitched quilt or apron made from old clothing; decoration, with what was at hand rather than from afar. Security was not how much you owned but what you could live without. This is the landscape of values in which I grew up, and it became one of the lenses through which I viewed the collections I encountered: some the result of careful consideration, others the consequence of mindless accumulation.

Collecting ranges in density from an occasional purchase to an addictive way of life. It might begin when a person inherits or purchases an interesting object—a duck decoy, an inkwell, a sampler—which leads to a second, similar purchase "because it goes with the one I have." Some collectors set limits and might say they want to own two or three paintings by Julian Onderdonk—perhaps his Texas landscapes with bluebonnets—or eighteenth-century furniture from Botetourt County, Virginia. When these collectors purchase a new piece, they often sell a lesser example in their collection. Good, I say.

For many people, a large collection is seen as an investment. If one etched Mettlach stein is a good investment, fifty of them are surely an outstanding asset. But this hope is often based on the erroneous assumption that as things get older, they get more valuable. The collectors who fifty years ago purchased pewter dinnerware, Hummel figurines, pump organs, pressed glass, and brass beds could attest to the fiction of this belief, as values for many of these have declined.

Collectors might also buy examples similar to pieces in their collection to "support the market." They may own five paintings similar to the one being offered and buy another to be sure that prices for that artist are not viewed as soft, thereby devaluing their collection. "I had to buy it."

On occasion, I worked with retired couples living in eight- or ten-room houses who had rented storage facilities because they "have nowhere to put anything."

Aside from the relatively straightforward collections of furniture, paintings, rugs, ceramics, glassware, and silver with which many homes are furnished, Brunk Auctions has sold collections of:

fine wine, miniature cloisonné, canoes, buttons, outsider art, dolls, Asian porcelains, tools (for woodworking, watchmaking, mining, assaying, prospecting, making instruments, blacksmithing, whaling, repairing machinery), Elvis and Beatles memorabilia, railroad lanterns, eighteenth-century iron hinges, movie posters, pocket watches, prosthetic glass eyeballs, Bakelite jewelry, baskets, quack medicine devices, coins, autographs, saddles and other western gear, Napoleonic memorabilia, walking sticks, animal figures (cats, dogs, owls, bats, horses, alligators, chickens, pigs, whales, snakes, possums, frogs, butterflies, sharks, birds), license plates, Japanese sword fittings, fashion hats, marble busts, pedal cars, daguerreotypes, Hummels, clocks, antique firearms and armor, pottery (English, Native American, prehistoric, Arts and Crafts, Southern folk, seventeenth-century German, ancient Roman), tobacco tags, books (literary works, fine bindings, horticultural, mysteries, sporting, decorative arts, entire libraries), Civil War memorabilia, scientific instruments (globes, barometers, microscopes, telescopes, medical, nautical, horological, survey instruments), tea equipage, African carvings, beer steins, toys, quilts, samplers, sewing equipment, rock and crystal specimens, masks, netsuke, country store tins, eighteenth-century insurance markers, lighting devices, marbles, musical instruments (guitars, violins, harps, concertinas, banjos, flutes, pianos, melodeons, harmonicas, autoharps, dulcimers), golf clubs and golf course passes, soldier figurines, maps, painted furniture, advertising signs, postcards, African American entertainment memorabilia, stamps, stagecoach hardware, art glass (Tiffany, Lalique, Steuben, Baccarat, Daum), ivory figures, 78 rpm records, christening dresses, unmounted diamonds and emeralds, candlesticks (brass, silver, iron, paktong, wooden), aviation and outer space collectibles, embroideries, stone and marble structures (fire surrounds, doorways, arcades, columns), chandeliers, photographs, metal and wooden models (locomotive, airplane, car, truck), baseball and football cards, beaded flappers. We have also sold (not as a collection) classic cars: Thunderbird, Porsche, Model T, Packard, Mercedes, Rolls-Royce, Daimler, Volvo.

We have declined to sell, for varying reasons, collections of bottle caps, paperback books, pencils, beer cans, sheet music, KKK and Nazi material, doorknobs, feathers, hubcaps, big game hunting trophies, medicine bottles, and the contents of a trailer park.

In 1988, we conducted an auction in rural Tennessee of a man's collection stored in several long chicken coops: forty-two pie safes, thirty-six beds, tools, sideboards, country store fixtures, advertising signs, stacks of tins removed from old ceilings, more than sixty chests, stacks of lumber, baskets, pottery, and over 1,200 chairs. Almost every car and truck fanning out across mid-Tennessee after our auction had chairs tied to its roof.

An estate in Brevard, North Carolina, was scattered through eight buildings. It took four auctions, two conducted by us and two by another firm, to sell everything: country furniture, glassware, baskets, toleware, typewriters, advertising tins, planters, barber chairs, adding machines, mounds of quilts and coverlets. One room in an old warehouse had eighteen pianos. The executors of the estate said the owner bought empty houses to provide storage for her collections.

What gives rise to this need to own and collect? I have it too. It began edging into my life when I first began going to auctions, one piece of pottery, one basket, one handmade chair at a time. I forsook my early mistrust of ownership. As the shelves filled, I created rationales to justify new acquisitions. "This basket was probably made in Virginia before 1900," or the best rationale, the one that covered almost everything I bought, "I'm helping preserve the material culture of the region."

Now there was joy and excitement in arranging rows of pottery on the dining room table to compare clay bodies, glazes, forms, and decorating techniques. Someone could have asked why I needed twenty pieces of pottery by the same maker. I had never been a potter, but when I examined what I had collected, I imagined digging the clay, turning a jar or vase, pitching slabs of wood into a groundhog kiln, seeing the red and yellow heat of the firing, and feeling the growing expectation of opening the still-warm kiln. Had the planets aligned to create a jar of great form and color? As I stood back and surveyed my collection, I realized that for a few moments, I had become a potter.

I could not have known that twenty years later, I would sell all my carefully gathered artifacts: pottery, baskets, paintings, books, Southern furniture, and folk art indigenous to Western North Carolina. I had lived a parallel life, selling things for others while buying things for my own collection, but never mixing the two.

A difficult divorce changed my life. The carefully vetted furniture, fine examples of regional pottery, and Southern Appalachian folk art that I'd once valued so deeply now had a diminished presence. It all felt slightly suspect. What could I count on? It seemed cumbersome and irrelevant to surround myself with hundreds of objects, no matter how carefully chosen or how incomplete my intended research. The pursuit of each handmade object, and the exploration of the social and cultural context that gave rise to each piece, had lost its vitality, its mystery.

Few of us choose to own nothing, and rarely do we read of someone who sells all their possessions and gives the proceeds to the poor. But I was gradually tempted by the idea of selling most of what I owned. I had imagined enjoying all of it in my old age—the Samuel Yellin ironwork, the fine leather-bound books—but maybe this was the time to clean house. Another letting go, the latest in a long series. The decision to sell my collections was not a sudden revelation, more the slow arrival of clarity. I sensed a brightness to it, perhaps an entrance.

To test myself, I took a favorite painting off the wall on which it had hung for fifteen years and put it in storage in our auction facility. How did that feel? Well, it felt fine. A few days later, two of my carefully chosen pieces of pottery left the blush of a spotlight on the shelf that had been their home and joined the painting in storage. This produced no adverse side effects. The slight flow from my house into storage became a steady stream. I paused many times as I watched myself packing and sorting, remembering the details of these pieces, now silent in boxes, wondering whether I would regret this decision.

A few months later, I sold everything I had collected, except one painting and one lamp, in one of my auctions, 636 lots. I prepared the catalog with care, including descriptive details and provenance when possible.

The auction was a relaxed affair. I had dealt with my anxieties several months earlier and was happy that my collection was well received. I enjoyed giving the history of many pieces and telling the stories of where I had found them. As was always the case at auctions, some pieces brought more than expected. Some less.

My two-story Tudor-style house, perched on a steep yard on Kimberly Avenue in Asheville, was now bare of all but basic essentials. One room echoed as I walked through. I felt lighter, more flexible, less obligated. If beauty was part of what I was after in assembling these collections, it would now need to be found in other venues. Had these objects been a source of comfort to me, tangible evidence of skill and intent? Had I somehow felt safer with all these things around me? I suffered no feeling of loss after they were gone.

All the rows of books, pottery, and carvings, the walls of prints and paintings, the stacks of ephemera and quilts, were statements to myself and to the world as to who I was and how I wished to be seen and understood. Perhaps I was a hunter and gatherer, a student and admirer of regional history and industry, or maybe I wished for my collection to suggest connoisseurship, skill in understanding and evaluating objects. But these personal icons may also have hidden what I was otherwise unable or unwilling to say about myself, messages I am still unable to identify. Why *had* I collected?

I embraced the new emptiness. I was back where I began many years earlier—a spare, undecorated Mennonite lifestyle—although my embrace lacked most if not all the attending theology.

I have often thought of a client, a woman of considerable wealth, who lived in the Asheville area and who in the summer of 1985 had invited me to come to her home to see if she had anything "we could use" in one of our auctions. At ninety-three, she lived alone, content and self-sufficient, and drove her car on errands around town. She had decided to move into assisted living in one of the many retirement centers in the area.

There was very little left in her house, as she had already made many decisions about which things would go to family members and which would be donated to a variety of local charities; small flags of multicolored paper indicated her carefully wrought choices. We chatted briefly about the few items she wanted me to look at, but the furniture we would have wanted for an auction had already been marked for other destinations. One piece, a fine, diminutive eighteenth-century English chest, had a bright pink tag with a note: "My granddaughter Esther." In the dining room was a group of three or four boxes and a short row of hangers with clothing, all marked in blue, "Take with me."

While I was there, a truck arrived from Habitat for Humanity to pick up several pieces she had donated: a mirror, bookshelf, rocking chair, large brass planter, a small table. She positioned herself beside the doorway, holding the door open with her slight body. As her donations were carried past her, she moved her hand slightly, guiding them through the doorway and out of her life.

She looked at me and said that the only things of real value to her were her family and friends and that the rest could just go to other people. "At the end, I just want to come out even."

RIFLE

On a chilly morning in February 1985, two years after I began my business, I drove the shoulderless, two-lane road from Asheville, North Carolina, to Johnson City, Tennessee, winding sixty miles through mountains and ravines and over the high ridge at the North Carolina–Tennessee line. The landscape bore the vestiges of failed farms and businesses: leaning barns with loose tin roofing; small, boarded-up grocery stores; lifeless trucks with bald, half-flat tires; bulldozers with spreading rust. A faded sign advertised a long-closed motel. A few white two-story farmhouses and the roads and schools—the largest employers in the area—gave the most evidence of sustained care. Trailers and pickup trucks huddled in the valleys, reflecting the slanting sun in the eastern sky. Sunken pumpkins and plastic Santa Clauses rested on porches. Flat layers of wood smoke slowly expanded in the still air. Every few miles, I passed a small steepled church and wondered where all the people who worshipped in these places might come from and what they believed.

Tom Kempson had called me a few days earlier to say he had attended an auction we'd conducted in East Tennessee and was interested in selling his collections. Several people had mentioned he had a houseful of great stuff, but in the shifting, often fickle markets for antiques and collectibles, I knew that not all "housefuls" made good auctions. I needed business, though, and was eager to see what he had.

Tom's residence was one of many small brick ranch houses in a weathered, 1950s neighborhood where several yards featured flat-lying tractor tires and large cast-iron pots filled with withered flowers. I was pleased to see

Tom's good-sized front yard and ample parking in his cul de sac, important ingredients for an on-site auction. A blue Ford pickup was parked in the short gravel driveway.

Tom met me at the front door. "Come in the house," he commanded as he swept one hand around the room in a great flourish, welcoming me to his exhibition. He was fifty or sixty years old, stocky, and dressed in outdoor gear. The rooms were crowded, every flat surface claimed by rows of glassware, figurines, and porcelains. The rooms smelled of lemon oil recently applied to oak furniture. He handed me an oak split basket made by Mary Prater of Calhoun County, Tennessee, the work remarkably detailed and perfectly executed. Years later, I too, would collect her exceptional baskets and other examples of Southern Appalachian folk art.

Tom opened a display case overflowing with pocket watches, medals, military ribbons, and pocketknives. Decoys, tobacco jars, advertising tins, lunch boxes, and Tennessee memorabilia were displayed on tables and shelves in other rooms. Tom had collected over thirty *Gone with the Wind* oil lamps, late Victorian double-globed lighting devices named after Margaret Mitchell's famous novel and often found in Southern collections. Clearly, there was enough material here for a full, one-day auction, and Tom's collection had the ingredients of a strong event: carefully gathered antiques, fresh to the market; a single owner rather than consignments from many people; and a front porch from which to sell his collection. This usually resulted in better attendance than an auction conducted in a rented hotel facility.

As we walked through the house, I evaluated my ability to catalog and advertise all that I saw. I felt sufficiently qualified until I saw several floor-to-ceiling cases crowded with rifles, muskets, fowling pieces, pistols, and revolvers, a mixture of nineteenth-century and modern firearms. I was raised in a Mennonite family with no guns of any kind. The only gun I'd ever owned was the 12-gauge shotgun I kept in the barn at our farm on Sugar Creek to entertain the crows that frequently destroyed my family's freshly planted garden. I felt a wave of uneasiness; could I promote and sell modern firearms? Though I had not been a member of a Mennonite church for many years, I still carried within me a grid of beliefs, or memories of beliefs; I wasn't sure which.

My Anabaptist (later known as Mennonite) ancestors of the sixteenth century refused to carry arms, backed away from confrontation, and stressed the importance of a nonresistant lifestyle, serving their fellow men. I didn't know how selling modern firearms fit with those traditions. Those

450-year-old Anabaptist articles of faith were still a slight but indelible current flowing under my life. They asked nothing of me, but these modern firearms reminded me again of their presence.

I didn't mention my Mennonite background to Tom and instead asked several general questions about his collection of firearms. He quickly sensed my apprehension and said with a slight smile that he would teach me everything I needed to know about the guns. He said this while rotating the cylinder of a Colt single-action revolver. Tom was justly proud of his collection of Tennessee rifles, a prominent feature of East Tennessee culture since William Bean, a maker of outstanding long rifles, settled at the convergence of the Watauga River and Boones Creek in 1769.

Many of Tom's rifles bore the signatures of their makers and carried long histories of ownership in Tennessee families, important provenance to prospector bidders and signs of a strong collection. These pieces would do well at auction since they were specific to person, time, and place—what most collectors of antiques watched for. There is a difference between, say, a handstitched quilt that was unmarked and the same quilt with information carefully stitched in one corner: "Alice Yoder / Mauganstown Maryland / 1847." I always enjoyed discovering these documented fragments of material culture, the rewarding but unpredictable archaeology of my work. These scarce artifacts were also the trophies that fueled the passions of collectors, many of them watching for traces of their own histories. Despite my reservations about the small group of modern handguns, I pushed aside the constraints of my personal history, convinced that my young business needed auctions like this to solidify our presence in Tennessee. I believed Tom could give me basic instruction on firearms and that we could work well together, creating a successful sale.

Three days later, I returned to Tom's house with a contract he quickly signed, and we began our work. He covered the dining room table with a blanket, laid an English flintlock musket in front of me, and stepped back with a smile, enjoying the prospect of becoming my teacher. The musket was dark and heavy. Its metal surfaces were crusty with age and had not been cleaned, always an asset in selling antique firearms.

We began with basic vocabulary: patch box, stock, pan, frizzen, forearm, lock, butt plate, barrel, rod. Here was the origin of the phrase "lock, stock, and barrel." Likewise, the phrase "flash in the pan": Tom explained that sometimes the powder in the pan of a flintlock rifle flashed when ignited by the spark but the gun failed to fire.

Next, Tom exchanged the flintlock with an early nineteenth-century percussion rifle, laying it gently on the table as though it were an offering placed on an altar. It was an East Tennessee long rifle with fancy brass mounts and detailed carving, striking evidence of skill and imagination. I picked up the rifle and sighted down the octagonal barrel. I was surprised by its balance and how well it fit my hands, arms, and shoulder. As I examined the initials scratched in cursive script on the top of the barrel, Tom told me the maker's name and when and where he had worked.

I asked if he thought there would be a lot of interest in his guns at the auction. "Aw, hell," he said with a fierce grin. "They'll be here like flies on roadkill."

Tom looked a bit like an old sailor, with a week-old beard, a stained cap, and a huge camouflage vest with bulging pockets. He discussed three generations of Bean Station rifle makers, their choice of woods, variations in their silver inlay, and the relation of their work to the Great Road migration down the Shenandoah Valley in the eighteenth and nineteenth centuries. Tom was as articulate and thorough as many formally trained scholars, perhaps more so in some cases. As we finished each gun, its lot number now waving on a small string tag, Tom would return the gun to the glass-doored cabinets and take out the next rifle or pistol. He shuffled back and forth and stood beside me while I asked questions and wrote descriptions. I learned about firing mechanisms, powder charges, caliber, and refinements in the design of firearms, improvements to make them more efficient.

When Tom went to the kitchen for a few minutes, I noticed a Colt Model 1911 .45- caliber, semiautomatic pistol with a seven-round magazine, a popular and widely produced weapon, lying on the table in front of me. I picked it up and removed the magazine. The gun fit my hand comfortably, the wooden grips worn from age and use. It had a kind of tactile clarity that encouraged touch and examination. Its moving parts slid and clicked with smooth precision.

I wanted to fire this gun, to hold it firmly with two hands, aim it at some benign target, and squeeze the trigger. I was startled by the seductive power this carefully designed instrument held for me, how quickly I wanted to fire it at something, the anticipation and release of confined energy, the small explosion that would change all my senses for a moment. I exhaled and laid down the gun.

When Tom returned, we continued our discussion of craftsmanship: how a gunsmith working at his forge in rural Tennessee in 1780 could make an impossibly straight barrel with only hand tools and a string; how the placement of the elements of a flintlock mechanism must work in perfect harmony to ignite the powder. These rifles were basic tools for survival in rural frontier life, like an ax or a plow point.

I worked at Tom's house almost every day for two months. I set up my lamp, camera, tape measure, magnifying glass, and reference books on a card table that we moved from room to room. I noted histories, descriptions, condition reports, and estimates on yellow legal pads. Tom carried things to the table and volunteered useful information. I was looking for details I could mention when the items were sold: this stoneware butter tub came from an estate sale in Greene County, Tennessee; or the cheek plate on this rifle is on the right side of the stock, indicating it was made for a left-handed man.

Our work gradually settled into a routine. I arrived at about eight thirty in the morning, and around nine o'clock, Tom would ask, in a friendly way, if I cared for a drink. I always declined. Then he, always standing at the kitchen sink, would produce a bottle of bourbon, gin, or vodka and pour a heavy splash into a glass, and we would proceed with our morning's work. He was always lucid and focused, but in the afternoons, usually around four o'clock, he would stretch and say he was going to take a nap, usually about the time the bottle was empty. I wondered if Tom's daily rituals at the kitchen sink would create problems during the auction.

We worked together day after day, examining each piece for the auction, both of us contributing to the discussion. Some days it seemed that a slight but distinct sense of trust existed between us, fragile but pleasant. I thought I saw it in his eyes: a more relaxed gaze, fewer quick glances.

Tom spoke very little about his life but occasionally alluded to episodes of violence he had survived. He often said, "I'm played out," or, "I been to tap city," a variation of being tapped out. He had driven a delivery truck for a few years and for "quite a while" had helped out in a hardware store. But primarily, he was active in an extensive and invisible economy that consisted of buying, selling, and making deals for antiques, guns, and ammunition. It was usually underground, mostly rural, and often dangerous. I had seen and heard signs of this well- embedded subculture, but this was the closest I had come to it. I learned not to ask questions.

Tom lived in fear of being assaulted: a gunman driving by and shooting into his house, or the nation being attacked by "A-rabs" or "Communists." Occasional news stories of gunmen entering schools or businesses and shooting strangers at random confirmed his worst fears. Tom had loaded guns in his truck, in the basement, beside his bed, and on his person.

One afternoon, we were working in one of the bedrooms, sorting his collection of dolls spread on a quilt-covered bed. Tom returned from a trip to the kitchen sink and settled heavily into a large walnut rocker. I was sitting beside the bed, using a reference book to look up marks on the heads and necks of porcelain dolls.

"You don't carry a gun, do you?" Tom asked. He looked directly into my eyes, his head tilted a bit to one side.

"No, I don't," I replied, setting my book aside. I suspected where this conversation was headed.

He said that most everyone around here carried a gun for protection and that you never know when you might need one. "What would you do if someone attacked your family?" he asked. "Would you just stand there?" He was outwardly calm but struggling to understand why I would not have a gun handy. His hands moved as he spoke, making slight rotations as his voice rose with his indignation.

Though I didn't know exactly what I would do, I explained, I would try to defuse the situation and defend my family as best I could. I would try to put myself between the attacker and my family and ask the attacker what he wanted. Was he after money?

"If you had a gun, would you shoot him?" Tom was trying to imagine not shooting the son of a bitch.

When I said I wasn't sure I would make good decisions if I had a gun, Tom shook his head slightly in disbelief.

"I would try to not respond with violence," was all I could say. Maybe I would grab a gun if someone was harming someone in my family. I didn't mention it, but a fellow auctioneer once recommended I not carry a gun, saying that if I had to use it, I would hesitate and might soon be dead. I knew Tom was not satisfied with my reasons for not carrying "protection." I had struggled to explain my rather vague beliefs but had been as honest as I could with him.

During the preview, the day before the auction, I wasn't thinking about what I would do if I were holding a gun. Collectors and antiques dealers began arriving from East Tennessee, Virginia, and North Carolina. Pickup trucks with Confederate flag license plates, heavily used vans pulling trailers, and repainted box trucks of uncertain age jockeyed for parking places in the cul-de-sac. Old friends greeted each other, chatting about their latest find. Several men and women poured over the Depression glass, naming patterns and rare colors.

Groups of men gathered around the gun collection. Barrel interiors were examined with tiny bore lights, serial numbers of Colt revolvers were checked for consistency, and cocking mechanisms were tested to see if they worked properly. Comments, directed at no one in particular but slightly louder than normal conversation, could be heard above the metallic rustle of their work.

"I think this sight has been moved. I wonder if the barrel has been shortened."

"I've never seen a trigger guard like this on a Tennessee rifle."

"This lock looks pretty shiny. I wonder if it's been replaced."

It was an old tactic—questions designed to raise doubts about the authenticity or value of the piece and hence discourage bidding. Some smiled when they heard them, carefully guarding their opinions with silence.

About midafternoon of the preview, I sought out Tom to help answer a question about a lamp. I found him parking his truck in a corner of his backyard where it joined a neighbor's fence. He was securing the auction site, wearing his familiar camo vest and cap. His manner was serious, almost grim, and he explained that if someone pulled a gun on the cashier, they would be blocked from escaping through the backyard. It had never occurred to me that we might be a target for a holdup.

The next day, auction day, was sunny and warm, a pleasant April morning. About a hundred people had spread out in the front yard with lawn chairs, coolers, and packing boxes. Many wore hats against a potentially hot afternoon sun. Tom and his wife, Dora, had made corn bread, ham biscuits, and coffee, which Dora sold at nominal prices from a table in the side yard. People waved to each other and shared bits of gossip or opinions about an upcoming piece. Tom patrolled the basement and backyard with periodic stops in the kitchen. I watched him take several things out of his vest and now understood his bulging pockets: they were full of ammunition. I was nervous about Tom, his trips to the kitchen, and the fears he harbored, fears against which he had armed himself so fully.

I stood on the small concrete porch behind two eight-foot folding tables, flanked by two loudspeakers on stands. Glassware, lamps, baskets, and furniture were brought out of the house by three or four runners. Small pieces were stacked briefly on the tables until held up to be sold, then replaced by more churns, advertising memorabilia, and porcelains. The antique firearms were sold at one o'clock. With Tom's coaching, I was able to describe the rifles accurately: "A fine brass-mounted half-stock curly maple percussion rifle with an ornate patch box and scrolled carving." Bidding was fast and spirited, with several rifles bringing over $5,000 each. An older man in bib overalls bid by holding his bid card high in the air, not moving it or looking at anyone until all others had pulled their cards down, their plans and courage extinguished by his resolve. This strategy, if repeated several times, might discourage competition and lead to bargains later in the day.

The last of Tom's collection, a pair of decoys, sold just before five o'clock. People paid their bills, helped each other load their trucks, and said goodbye to their friends. Tom watched my wife, Jan, the cashier, prepare the deposit for the bank; he stood with both hands stuck inside his vest. Two of our crew, one of whom carried a gun, left for the night deposit drawer of a local bank with the proceeds of the auction, slightly over $80,000. Our crew of ten, some bending to fill large black plastic bags, finished cleaning up the house and yard. I thought of shaking hands as we were about to leave, but Tom was not the hand-shaking kind.

Our caravan of five or six vehicles headed home through Johnson City, then climbed the winding road from Flag Pond up to Sam's Gap at the Tennessee–North Carolina line, past old tobacco barns, clotheslines hung with quilts for sale, and narrow, three-pump gas stations. At the crest of the ridge, cars and trucks often pulled over onto a large apron of gravel to cool their motors before plunging down the steep grade on either side. As I approached the apron, the driver of a pickup truck waved me over. Not until he got out did I recognize Tom. How strange, I thought, that he would follow me to the North Carolina line.

He walked over to my car, still wearing his bulging vest. He said he wanted to talk to me a moment. I got out and leaned against my car. A tremor of fear had stiffened my legs. Tom stood in a posture of readiness, his legs slightly spread, his camo cap shading his eyes from the bright evening sun. We discussed the auction briefly, both agreeing it had gone well. Then, staring at the ground, he said, "Bob, I know you're an honest man. But I don't trust anyone, and I'm gonna have to frisk you."

He wanted to be sure I wasn't stealing the money. He had told many stories of how he had been deceived and cheated by people he traded with; there was no auctioneer in the state of Tennessee he trusted.

"Tom, you go ahead if you need to," I said, relieved. I explained that the money was in the bank back in Johnson City but that he probably had no reason to trust me any more than anyone else. I held my arms out at my sides. He waited a bit, then took a step toward me. One hand just touched my shirt. Then he stopped. He looked directly at me with his head tilted a bit, then dropped both his hands, took a step back, turned, and walked to his truck.

This is how, late one afternoon in April 1985, at Sam's Gap on the Tennessee–North Carolina line, Tom Kempson, against all his instincts, armed with a gun and a vest full of ammunition, let go of a single strand of his tightly woven fear and mistrust. The step he took, backwards, was in the best tradition of my Mennonite past, something one of my Anabaptist ancestors might have done.

UMBRELLA

In the late 1970s, several years before I became an auctioneer, I began attending Franklin's Auction, located several miles northwest of downtown Asheville. One Friday night, Jake Shipley, one of the auctioneers, was selling an old faded umbrella to a full house of auction goers. Since he often bought the remnants of a yard sale for a few dollars, then ran the goods through the auction, the umbrella was undoubtedly his.

The bidding had stalled at one dollar, Jake flailing away, trying to get another bid. One of the floor workers opened and closed the umbrella and spun it around to show it was intact. Suddenly, the bidding had a new urgency, many people now interested in the faded blue umbrella with a curved wooden handle. The bidding slowly rose in fifty-cent increments to ten dollars, then twenty. Five or six people still had their bid cards in the air. Ambient conversation stopped. Everyone was watching, several people cheering as the next bid was taken. James Anderson stood at the back of the room, his hands on his hips, a faint, knowing smile slowly working its way across his anxious face. He knew what was about to happen.

Jake was so excited he could hardly get the next number out, but the bidding continued, steady and solid. At fifty dollars, Jake switched to one-dollar increments, his face blotchy red as he wheezed for air. His mind may have raced back to other times when things he was selling brought shocking prices: the $430 quilt, the $1,100 painting, the $650 cut glass bowl. He didn't know the reasons why things sometimes brought so much, and he didn't care, just as he didn't care why the umbrella was suddenly so valuable. If these people believed it was valuable, that was their problem.

At sixty dollars, the bidding finally ended, and Jake, who couldn't believe his good fortune, stood and announced, smiling and pointing at the bidder, "Sold, sixty dollars to number thirty-seven." Then, number thirty-seven—a grinning older woman—and most everyone else in the crowded room, including James Anderson and me, stood up and yelled, "Happy birthday, Jake!" All were clapping, laughing, slapping backs, except Jake, whose sixty dollars had evaporated in the eruption of hot, blinding noise.

Earlier that evening, James Anderson and I had been standing in the gravel parking lot of Franklin's Auction. James's watery eyes were sprung wide open, dried saliva in the corners of his mouth. He walked slowly, as though in fear of being surprised. Some were suspicious of his strange ways and believed he was heavily medicated. He drifted through the countryside in search of bargains, a picker who now stood beside me. Franklin's Auction was a refuge for James; here, people accepted him and his halting efforts to make a living.

James said quietly that he had something he wanted to show me.

"Whatcha got?" I asked. James occasionally found a good piece of folk art.

"You better come look." His eyelids fluttered as he searched for words.

His green van was overflowing, the interior so jammed there was room only on the front seats for him to press himself against a pile of clothing and used food containers. I could see a protruding bicycle wheel, part of an armchair, shovel handles, rugs, an old radio. Two metal yard chairs and a TV antenna, upright between them, were tied on the roof. This arrangement, makeshift as it was, did suggest display, intent.

A stepladder, a rusty Coca-Cola cooler, a partial set of golf clubs, and the top of a cider mill bulged out the open back doors, held by a web of worn clothesline. In traffic, the battered green van always drew stares, as though it had been in a wreck of some sort. Out of earshot of James, some auction goers said his van was itself a work of outsider art. I suspected it was also his home.

He reached through the open window on the passenger side and pulled out a river cane basket, lacking most of its bottom. "I know you like Cherokee baskets," he said as he handed it to me. He had seen me pay twenty-six dollars for a Cherokee basket several weeks earlier. He lit up a Marlboro, his hands shaking.

I said that I did like them but that they needed to be in better shape: "This one's too far gone." I admired fine baskets by makers of both European and

Cherokee descent and arranged them—oak split, honeysuckle, and river cane—on shelves, imagining the skill of their makers.

"You can have it for four dollars." His voice just short of urgent.

I told him I would pass on this one but to keep me in mind if he found other good baskets or pottery. We walked across the gravel toward the unpainted one-story cinder block building where the auction was about to begin.

.....

In 1970, our family of four—my wife, Jan, our two children, Ingrid and Andrew, aged three and two, and me—had moved to a deserted farm in a community called Sugar Creek, in the mountains of North Carolina. We were back-to-the-land people; I supported our family as a woodworker, making furniture and puzzles in the old farmhouse. I worked long days, hauling logs to the sawmill, cutting precise dovetails, driving to craft fairs throughout the Southeast and selling my wares to make enough money to support our family. I began going to auctions to buy furniture to study construction techniques and design elements.

Franklin's Auction was in the section known as Emma, rolling terrain populated with small, mostly part-time farms and a scattering of mobile homes, some with pickup trucks and boats parked nearby. The area may have been named after Emma Clayton, wife of Thomas Clayton, who in the nineteenth century ran a sawmill off the creek flowing through the area.

David and Ada Franklin, whom I guessed to be in their late sixties or early seventies, ran an honest, friendly auction, no imaginary bids taken off the back wall. David had a fatherly style and smoked a pipe, which he often pointed at bidders. Ada stood at the front of the room, usually smiling, keeping order over the proceedings, calling out the number of the consigner for each item as it came up to be auctioned. "This is on number eight," she would say, turning to the clerk.

Every Friday night, the regulars gathered: Martin Phillips, the florist, who loved Asian ceramics and enamels; Miss Silver, who often wore a purple polka-dot dress and bought used furniture for her store on Lexington Avenue; the man who collected Victorian glass and Occupied Japan ceramics and bid by waving across his face as though chasing a pesky insect; the lady who bid on all dolls, her iridescent hair the orange of broiled lobster; the gruff old man, always hunched over in his chair, who bought tools and bid by saying, "Uh-huh"; Mr. Steinberg, who often bought new and used suitcases. And James Anderson, always there, watching when a piece or two of his was being sold. Some regulars never bid on anything; it was just the best way they knew to spend Friday evenings.

Every item that came up for auction held secrets: What is it? What is it worth? Could I sell it for a profit? To whom? My embrace of those tiny mysteries was what I held in common with all the people in the room, all of us on the road to Canterbury, pilgrims in search of miracles of any size.

Children chased each other between chairs. People ate hot dogs, read newspapers, bragged about their latest find, asked where Fred was tonight. Some stood with their arms folded and bid casually while they talked to other people. Some labored over each twenty-five- or fifty-cent increase in the bidding. Many were the owners of what was up for auction. There were no phone or Internet bidders, written programs, buyer's premiums, or catalogs; people had things to sell, and here was a small congregation of buyers. The only issue to be decided was the price, commerce at its most basic.

Almost everyone, including me, smoked; many chewed tobacco; some both. The air in the building varied from a slight haze to a heavy fog: people coughed and rattled. Across the fence from the yellow school buses used for storage at the back of the parking lot, in a neighbor's pasture, sat several muddy, slapped-together pig sheds that produced a powerful odor. On a hot summer evening with a slight westerly breeze, the pig air drifted into the auction house like a dark tide, rendered slightly less offensive by the cigarette smoke.

It was colorful, improvised theater, and I was soon drawn in. I stood there almost every Friday night and became one of the cast, the tall guy, not from around here, looking for something. Soon, I became one of the sellers, taking in a load of what I found each week at yard sales and flea markets, watching my merchandise sell on Friday night, then on Monday morning collecting my money and Mrs. Franklin's careful listing of what I had sold. How encouraged I was in my scavenging when something I bought for ten dollars sold for fifteen or twenty dollars.

There was much for me to learn. One way to boost bidding on any electrical item was to reassure the crowd that it ran. Mrs. Franklin plugged in vacuum cleaners, electric drills, fans, and hair dryers, and Mr. Franklin or Jake Shipley, the two auctioneers, would announce, "You can hear it running." Language was critical; they did not say the device worked or did what it was supposed to do. As long as it made some sort of sound, a slight whir or a little vibrating hum, it passed.

One night, I bought a brass desk lamp. I had not looked at it before the auction began, a common error, but I could picture it on my desk, solid and adjustable. That visualization of what a thing might be and how it might look in another setting would eventually get me in trouble, a small demon of my own making.

Jake Shipley sold the lamp to me for $1.50. He was not a social enabler; he was wired to the numbers, pounding for every possible bid. Some said he beat things to death. I had stopped bidding at $1.00, and the last bid had been $1.25. Jake, grinning, had looked at me and said, "A quarter more and it's yours." I nodded. The lamp was handed to me as soon as I bought it, a flimsy, cheap thing held together by an improvised bolt. The amp was made of a low-grade base metal with only a thin, worn layer of brass plating. Since I had not looked at the lamp beforehand, I knew it was my fault but decided to protest anyway. I waited until the auction was over, about two hours later, to talk to Jake Shipley.

I walked up to the small stage where Jake was sitting. He lit up a Winston and turned to me with a broad smile.

"Son, how you gettin' along?" he asked, friendly to a new face in the small crowd. "We're sure glad to see you coming to the auctions," he said, as though it were some kind of church service. "What sort of stuff you lookin' for?"

I said nothing special, just looking for a bargain like everyone else, but I did have a question about this lamp I had bought. I explained that the lamp was not brass but a base metal with a thin layer of brass plating. I held out the lamp toward him.

He never looked at the lamp. Still smiling, he said, "No, I said it was brass-lookin', and it does look like brass to me."

But I was not deterred by this vocabulary lesson. Underlying the sale of each box of musty linens and each dim painting lay a tiny drama, the possibility that this thing was rare and valuable. Conversations were spiked with talk of great finds, real or imagined: the old chair that turned out to be an American Chippendale example from coastal Virginia; a rare piece of New Jersey glass signed Dorflinger, found in a box of miscellaneous glassware. The intrigue of a valuable discovery was always with me. On several occasions, I even flipped through a large old book, hoping for the mythic twenty-dollar bill hidden in its pages. I was seduced by this contagion, the pursuit of unrecognized treasure, low-stakes gambling.

The rise of this curiosity in my life was permanent and drove my buying, selling, and collecting; eventually, it led to my becoming an auctioneer.

About a month later, in a box of miscellaneous silver, I found several sewing implements attached to a belt. I learned that this was known as a chatelaine, a French word for a small clasp or chain, often silver, worn on the waist by women, often the mistress of a castle, and used to carry keys, a watch, or other implements, popular in the seventeenth through the nineteenth centuries. Even though my chatelaine was a later copy of an old one, I found some pleasure in learning this and logged it away in the growing constellation of similar particles of information. The more arcane and obsolete the object, the more I was attracted to it: stoneware ant traps, cheroot pistols, sugar nippers, post presses. I was interested in the origin of these artifacts and the language used to describe them, a mix of archaeology, etymology, and cultural history. Increasingly, I bought with the idea of reselling to make a profit.

In the months that followed, I took home from my expanding route of weekend auctions handwritten Civil War era letters, old theater costumes, handwrought iron tools, porcelain figurines, pressed glass, quack medicine devices, pewter chargers, old photos and maps. I bought boxes for the pleasure of examining and sorting them, on one occasion a box of handwritten ledgers, letters, and business records from the long-closed Hans Reese Tannery in Asheville. I read through these documents slowly, imagining the people and their lives in Asheville in the 1890s.

Ingrid and Andrew, then preteens, often helped me sort through the boxes, usually on the dining room table. Jan dreamed of a clean, modern decor. Boxes of auction rubble spread on the plywood floor of the A-frame house I had built was not what she had in mind. But she was patient with my current passion of digging through boxes, especially since Ingrid and Andrew were involved.

We sifted and organized postcards, costume jewelry, tobacco tags, old toys, 78 rpm records, and country store tins. We especially enjoyed jars of buttons. We laid the bone, mother-of-pearl, ivory, and glass specimens in rows; the brass buttons worn by police, firemen, sailors, or conductors got special attention. We found a set of enameled plique-à-jour buttons, each of a different bird—fine jewelry worn by a famous person, we speculated. One evening, we found an 1890s brass button marked "Albany Police" and invented stories about how the button got from Albany, New York, to a box in Franklin's Auction near Asheville, North Carolina, almost a hundred years later. Or was the button from Albany, Georgia? When Ingrid and Andrew accompanied me on my trips to craft fairs to sell my woodworking, we kept an eye out for antique shops where we might find a jar of buttons to sort through while we traveled.

About three years into the business of buying and selling, I traveled to Philadelphia, New York, and Boston to attend auctions at Freeman's, Christie's, Skinner's, and other prominent auction houses. What began as colorful entertainment on Friday nights gradually became a serious business: we had mortgage and health insurance bills to pay. I strung together a network of dealers and collectors to sell to. Many pieces went to my booth at the Corner Cupboard Antiques Mall in downtown Asheville. I also opened a booth at Farmstead Antiques, near Winston-Salem, North Carolina. I was in full swing: buy it for fifty dollars, sell it for eighty dollars; buy it for twenty dollars, sell it for thirty-five.

I learned the heft of bronze, much heavier than spelterware with a bronze finish. I took brass andirons apart to see if the interior rod was handwrought. I looked for the seesaw evidence of pit-sawed lumber, for the dots of offset printing on framed works of art, for pontil scars on blown glass. Now I carried a magnifying glass in my pocket, to examine the minute landscapes of use: texture, wear, color changes, signs of repair.

ELEVATOR

A well-dressed woman entered the antiques shop. She walked over to a wall of gilt accessories, took a tape measure from her purse, and measured the interior of a small frame. She knew the owner, Robert Young, and was here now to double-check her measurements. She approached him with an offer for the frame, priced at $2,250, and spoke in a slightly condescending manner as she held her glasses beside her cheek. "Mr. Young," she announced in a brittle, unattractive voice, "I will give you $1,700 for this frame. I think I might be able to use it."

Mr. Young thundered back, "Lady, the price is $2,500 to you, and if you ask again, the price will be $3,000. If you don't like my prices, you can get out of my store." He was victorious and unrepentant as he watched her quickly head for the door.

On this cool, windy fall morning in 1982, I had decided to visit Mr. Young despite his reputation for being cranky and unpredictable. His cavernous shop sat in an old building about three stores down from Pack Square in downtown Asheville. Parking was plentiful that day, the booming profusion of galleries, boutiques, and restaurants still thirty years in the future.

Just inside the door, I paused to look at an immense stone wellhead, rusty iron fittings still embedded in the stone. But as soon as he saw me, Mr. Young, seated near the rear of the store, leaped to his feet and stomped toward me. "Can I help you?" he asked sharply, sizing me up.

"I'm a friend of Jerry Israel," I replied; Jerry did all the advertising for Mr. Young's estate auctions. I was considering becoming an auctioneer, and Jerry suggested I get to know Mr. Young, since his shop would be an easy way for me to get exposure to a lot of fine antiques. I hoped it might also help me define the sort of business I imagined for myself. Jerry and I sang in the same shape note singing group, and I often turned to him for his encyclopedic knowledge of local history and traditions. He became a trusted resource for counsel on how to create and sustain the auction business and later worked for Brunk Auctions for several years. He had special gifts when working with clients: he was always patient, and helpful.

Mr. Young quickly realized that I was not a serious buyer. "Oh yes, well, just look around. You can go upstairs on the freight elevator. It cost me $1,800 to get the goddamned thing fixed," he shouted, retreating to his desk.

In his mid-eighties, he was short and dressed for business, his suit coat hanging over the back of his desk chair. He wore a Scottish tartan vest, the arc of his gold pocket watch chain visible near a lower pocket. He was bald and had a mark shaped like a small bolt of lightning across his forehead. The scar, caused by a difficult case of shingles, remained pale white when his face was flushed in anger. His glasses hung on a lanyard around his neck. Jerry had told me that one of Mr. Young's best friends called him a "banty rooster."

I went back to look at the wellhead more carefully. The massive square carved stone base—one piece—sat heavily on the gritty oak floor, as if resting from the exertion of getting there: a monolith of sorts, speckled with traces of dark green lichen, the iron a cloudy black with scattered rust stains.

A tall, four-legged iron structure, the overthrow, was embedded in the top of the stone base. Its legs curved in at the top and were joined just above a pulley from which hung a fragment of chain, if complete, would have made it possible to raise and lower a bucket into the round entrance to the well below.

I pictured people in a small Italian village, several hundred years earlier, gathered around this well, buckets in their hands, grateful for clean water protected by the wellhead. Some leaned against the stone base as they lowered their vessels. I imagined myself there on a sunny fall day, laughing with my neighbors.

I slowly relinquished my visit to the tranquil Italian village to investigate other pieces Mr. Young was selling. I walked up to an oversize Gothic Revival armchair, perhaps from a church; the price tag marked $12,000. Then a Chinese coromandel screen, $24,000, and an oversize English partner's desk, $18,000. To me, Mr. Young's prices were unimaginably high, eight or ten times more than I would have expected in my small world of buying and selling antiques.

I examined several pieces of furniture and came to what was labeled a Hepplewhite sideboard, a twentieth-century reproduction of a furniture design popular in the early nineteenth century. I realized that when Mr. Young said Chippendale or Hepplewhite, he was referring to a furniture style and did not necessarily mean the piece had been made in the eighteenth or nineteenth century, a distinction he either had not fully explored or chose to ignore. Mr. Young's success as a merchant did not seem to be based on scholarship, as I had assumed. Rather, it appeared to be grounded in his commitment to offering impressive merchandise, with equally remarkable prices.

I had no experience with the ormolu-mounted French furniture in Mr. Young's shop, or the belle époque bronzes, eight-by-ten-foot tapestries, or paintings of classical ruins, with cherubs in the upper corners holding drapery. I wondered if I could negotiate the cultural distance between my spare, conservative Mennonite background and the world of formal antiques. My ancestors' dreams did not include ownership of Italianate paintings mounted in Florentine gilt frames, their sense of artistic merit more likely enlivened by a finely stitched quilt or, in a freshly plowed field, with perfectly spaced furrows as far as one could see.

....

The Mennonite churches of my childhood gave me little exposure to fine architecture and decorative arts. Though I grew up in Chicago, our family often visited two of my mother's sisters, Aunt Stella and Aunt Ada, who lived on large farms near Sterling, Illinois. While there, we always "went to church" at the Science Ridge Mennonite Church, a white-painted frame structure cornered on three sides by cornfields.

As a child, I stared at the rows of oak benches and a small stage and pulpit beside which the chorister stood while leading the congregational singing. Men sat on the left side of the sanctuary, women on the right; infant children were usually held, as there was no nursery. The walls were painted white, as colors other than white were considered too secular. This also accounted for the absence of a piano or organ: too "worldly." No stained glass window, statuary, ornament, or decoration graced the interior of the sanctuary; only a small cross could be seen behind the pulpit. We were here to worship, not to look around the room.

I did find a bit of ornament in the pages of the *Mennonite Hymnal* from which we sang during all worship services. It would be years before

I learned to read music, but I watched carefully as each of these notes and the strange shapes at the top of each vertical stem spread across the pages. I was also attracted to the texture and harmonies created by the four lines of music: soprano, alto, tenor, and bass voices, not accompanied by any instruments. This tradition of four-part congregational singing has informed my life for many years as I still sing music of this kind on a regular basis. I always enjoyed singing in church, even when the sermons were endlessly boring.

Later, as a teenager, I paid more attention to clothing. The women of this congregation, and the other conservative Mennonite women of my youth, wore black or brown shoes but no jewelry or makeup, their legs unshaven. Their shapeless dresses were designed to extinguish the lustful hopes of any wayward eyes, including mine.

.....

I needed to create a new frame of reference for myself, a new vocabulary. I had to imagine how other people, often wealthy people, would look at an object: what they saw, what activated their senses and their desire to own.

I walked over to the wellhead again. When I first entered the shop, it struck me as a bit out of place, a clumsy, rusty object, heavy, hard to move. But I realized that it was in several ways the most interesting piece in Mr. Young's shop. A commanding stone wellhead to feature in your curated English flower garden, or to place beside the small stream, near the stone terraces flanking the entrances to your estate. The piece people would walk up to and ask about, the only stone wellhead around.

Mr. Young knew instinctively that this was an exceptional object. I wanted to have that awareness, that intuition when I encountered a stellar object to not brush past something foreign to me. I needed to become fluent in a wide range of aesthetic and decorative tastes, even if I didn't know exactly when and where a piece was made.

The idea of becoming an auctioneer seemed to be taking root. I liked the prospect of examining objects as cultural expressions born of specific times and places and their histories of ownership. What values and beliefs gave rise to the existence of this object?

Why would people wish to own a dented silver spoon or a badly worn rug?

I didn't imagine myself flogging crowds to get another bid, but I thought I might be able to learn how to put useful information in front of people.

I browsed through both floors of Mr. Young's shop for an hour. As I left, I thanked him for letting me look around. He stood up and asked flatly, "What are you going to do?"

I wasn't certain what he meant; I certainly wasn't going to buy anything.

"Well, are you going to have an antique shop?" He said I couldn't sell anything unless I had a good way to sell what I bought. "Are you going to be an auctioneer?" he gestured adamantly as he asked. I realized Jerry must have told him my tentative plans.

"I have a booth in an antique mall, but I've been thinking about getting my auctioneer's license. I made furniture for a number of years, but I'm not really sure what I'm going to do next."

He ended the conversation, saying, "Well, all right," and sat down.

A month or two later, on a cold winter day, I stopped by to see him again. As I entered the shop, I saw a large red "Sold" sign hanging from the top of the Gothic armchair, now displayed in a front window. Mr. Young wore a tweedy suit and, with no customers in sight, was sound asleep in his office chair, his body a straight diagonal line from the floor to his head. He had covered himself up to his chin with newspapers to ward off the chill. I walked around making intentional noise at the other end of the shop so he could awaken in relative privacy. I heard the rattle of newspapers as he stirred. He marched down the center of the shop. "What can I do for you?" he half shouted. As I turned around, he said, "Oh, it's you, well, OK then," slowing as he came near, disappointed again that I was not a serious buyer.

A little later, three women entered the shop and began looking at dining room chairs. One of the women was soon conducting a loud lecture on Chippendale chairs, which she pronounced "cha-yuhs," and had the attention of two or three other shoppers. Mr. Young was furious and approached her quickly as soon as he realized she was a distraction. "Which of these Chippendale chairs do you intend to buy?" he shouted. Flecks of spit flew from his lips. He didn't wait for an answer. "These fine people are interested in several things here, and if you want to just talk, you'll need to go outside."

As they left, he turned to me as though he now regarded me as a confidant of sorts—not as a good friend, more like a small audience he could count on. "She's been in here before but never buys anything. How does she expect me to make any money? It's not easy to find good stuff anymore," he railed, in real or feigned anger. It would be a while before I could tell the difference; maybe there was no difference.

How could he run a business like this? I wondered. I couldn't imagine yelling at customers, running someone out of a shop. But they put up with him; there was nowhere else in the area to shop for period gilt frames or sets of Chippendale-style chairs.

His explosions of anger struck me as performance, improvisations he could call forth to defend his territory and assert his authority. Adult tantrums.

Mr. Young's family had lived in Asheville for several generations. His father, Jonas Young, had owned a brick business and supplied the bricks for part of the Confederate jail constructed in Statesville, North Carolina, during the Civil War. Mr. Young shared many of the values and folkways of the region, particularly a dislike of pretense. But there was irony in his impatience with posturing, as he excelled at creating illusions himself.

Many people enjoyed telling "Mr. Young stories," particularly examples of his colorful vocabulary. Jerry and I were in his shop one day just after Mr. Young had sold a consigned sideboard for a great deal of money and, speaking of his client, predicted, "He'll be as happy as a dog with two dicks."

Mr. Young had created a caricature of himself, the feisty old man and his fine antiques, the alarming prices, the outrageous language, his shop a landmark in Asheville. The stories people told about him only added to the mystique—and for some, the charm—of it all.

In the years that followed, I gradually understood the reasons for his high prices. If you needed a six-foot fire fender or a table that could accommodate eighteen guests, there was no other place in the area where you might find such things. There are many large and historically important homes in Western North Carolina, and Mr. Young had their owners directly in his sights. He was keenly up to date on the antiques trade in New York and other urban centers and made no apology for his prices. Mr. Young sold most of the great collections from the wealthy estates in the area and knew many of the owners.

Robert Young offered the grand and the impressive, objects that would make a heroic statement in your home. He had no time for the residue of rural life—no pie safes, baskets, pottery, or butter churns in sight. There were also no freshly cut flowers, bowls of potpourri, or other decorator flourishes: this was an arena for serious buyers looking for significant improvements in how they presented themselves to the world. Mr. Young's wife, Ann, his full partner in all his ventures, was often at work in the shop, restoring a large gilt frame; and at any time, there might be a piano tuner working on a grand piano. It resembled a museum storage room, exactly what Mr. Young intended.

Later, when I was an active auctioneer, Mr. Young would occasionally offer advice. "Brunk," he began one day as we sat in his shop, "the most important thing for you to do is live longer than your buyers." He explained that when the people who come to your auctions get old or die, they or their family will call you to sell their things if you're still alive. Mr. Young knew whereof he spoke. At age ninety-two, he had outlived many of his buyers and was still in his shop, saying, "My dear, have you seen this fine Sheraton sideboard?" or, "If you want to look upstairs, take the freight elevator."

When Mr. Young decided to go out of business in 1994, he asked us to conduct the auction of what remained in his shop. He had stopped buying major pieces for inventory, and what was left were only remnants of the outstanding offerings for which he was known. Long gone were the twelve-foot bookcases, the four-foot andirons, the paintings of classical ruins, the wellhead. But many old friends came to the auction and traded favorite stories.

I had witnessed one of these episodes myself. It occurred when he was selling an old, bedraggled chest in one of his estate auctions. A woman in the front row, interested in bidding on the chest, listened as Mr. Young praised its many outstanding features. She stood up, her entanglement of bright red hair shaking as she shouted, "Mr. Young, it's missing a drawer!"

Mr. Young, in an equally strident voice, replied, "Lady, when you are as old as this chest, you'll be missing your drawers too." I wanted to remember this story so I could repeat it in case I ever sold a piece of furniture missing a drawer.

We held the auction in his shop, still three doors down from Pack Square. Mr. Young found it difficult for someone else to be in charge of an auction in his shop—or, for that matter, anywhere else—and even though we negotiated potential problems with relative goodwill, often with help from Jerry or Ann, I was apprehensive that a spasm of anger stemming from some slight of his authority might erupt.

And I was worried about the gun he had shown me on several occasions, clearly visible in his right front pants pocket the morning of the auction. I asked Jerry if he thought Mr. Young would actually use the gun if some confrontation broke out. Jerry smiled and said that several years earlier, Ann had a friend file off the firing pin on the hammer of Mr. Young's revolver.

Mr. Young had never conducted an auction using computers, but we used the fledgling technology and set up a computer near the front door to register people for the auction. His staff had always registered people by hand and used the card system to keep track of purchases. He eyed our computer and asked curtly, "Are you going to use that thing?" I replied that we had found it very helpful in organizing our work. He said no more and walked away. Our computer and printer, PA system, lights, and other electronic devices were more than the old wiring in the shop could accommodate. About ten minutes before the auction began, our computer let out a well-defined puff of smoke and smoldered to a halt. So, for his last auction, we used Mr. Young's old handwritten card system.

WHEELBARROW

The language was hobbled and fused into new words:
"Now would you bid?" became *nominabid.*
"Do you want them at?" became *wanamat.*
"Will you bid?" became *willybidda, erdabid,* or *illabider.*
"Do you want them for five?" became *wanamafive.*
"I believe I would" became *blevawood.*

To string the words and numbers together in a smooth line also required cadence and the sound *nuh* (now) to create syncopation; thirty, thirty, thirty, *nuhthirty,* thirty. Sixty became *sickity,* seventy became *senny,* smoothing out the nonmelodic consonants and wrong-syllabled words. It helped me to understand this as a form of music: the rhythm and cadence as the ground, the words as a melody of sorts, sung allegro (fast and lively) or as an ostinato (a short repeated pattern). *Senny, senny, senny nuh senny, no eighty, no eighty, noweighty, noweighty, say eighty, nuh niney, niney niney nuh niney, wanamat niney, hunnert, hunnert, hunnert nuh hunnert, say hunnert?*

To become a licensed auctioneer in North Carolina, I had two choices: apprentice with a licensed auctioneer for two years or take a two-week course at an accredited auction school, either of which would qualify me to take the licensing exam. I had chosen an auction school because it was faster and now, in the fall of 1982, found myself seated with thirty-five other students.

I had been a student at Princeton Seminary for a year, earned a graduate degree in social work, taught sociology at UNC Asheville for four years, and been a farmer and woodworker, but now, at the age of forty, the auction business looked like the best fit so far for my interests and aptitudes. But this was not the refinement of a career search of existing agencies or employment possibilities. I wanted to create something of my own invention—a new way to define myself—and live responsibly in this world. I anticipated careful research, creative marketing, improvised theater, long hours, inevitable failures. I was eager to throw myself into a new challenge and embrace its mysteries and risks.

Auction school encouraged the mystique of the chant, the singsong, fast-talking style of calling for bids. State and national auctioneer championships were based on the smoothness and uniqueness of the chant. In the rural South, the auctioneer is part cowboy, farmer, old-fashioned horse trader, con man, and, above all, preacher. The auctioneer's chant is close to rhythmic Pentecostal preaching, the "uh" after many words: "The time-uh for salvation is now-uh." At auction school, hours were spent learning to talk quickly. We were handed a microphone wrapped in a red bandanna and instructed to count backwards from $165.00 in $2.50 increments as fast as possible, evenly, and without hesitation.

As I traveled in my car or truck, I sold cows, streetlights, fence posts, interstate signs, and tires, always ending by singing, "And I sold it for a thirty-dollar bill" to a long-remembered sequence of notes in Gregorian chant, closer to my taste in chants. I would make each utility pole or every third white center line a bidding increment so that turns and intersections required adjusting the cadence. I played tapes of national champion livestock auctioneers; the best were clear, percussive, melodic.

Evenings at auction school, students would gather and discuss the day's session. Most were men, one a Black minister hoping to raise money for his church. Some wanted to become contract auctioneers for added income on weekends. Others focused on selling real estate or livestock, or on opening a general merchandise Friday night auction. Several clearly struggled with a lack of sustaining resources. All, like me, were considering a substantial shift in their lives.

At the time, our family lived on our mountain farm north of Asheville. Four or five students in auction school with rural backgrounds reminded me of several of our neighbors on Sugar Creek. They lived close to the ground and were ready to help, solid and steady. My kind of people.

As the parade of professional auctioneers rolled through the days at auction school, I learned many responses to stalled bidding—words to cajole, flatter, scold, or encourage when the bidding stopped. I liked these phrases; they personalized the proceedings a bit and offered opportunities for friendly humor. Depending on the setting, I used variations of these for many years:

Stay with me now.

That lady knows what she's doin'.

You were doing so well.

We're selling it, not renting it.

You're allowed to bid twice, you know.

Think of this as a great anniversary gift.

It's your turn.

Don't go home and say there weren't any bargains.

One session at auction school was led by an attorney who explained the basic elements of contracts so we would be prepared for questions about them when they appeared on the state licensing exam. Bid calling and bidding create legally binding oral contracts. "Would you pay one hundred dollars for this item?" If the answer is "Yes," in whatever form that takes, a contract exists. Mortgages, tobacco, livestock, fine jewelry, cars, US Treasury bills, heavy equipment, real estate, and wheat futures are all sold at auction, each industry with its own rituals and carefully honed signals and vocabularies. Most of these specialized auctions are attended by professional buyers, usually not the general public.

In the years that followed my time at auction school, I learned that bidding at auctions can take many forms: the slight nod, the anxious wave, the touched nose or ear, the twitched finger. Stories like the one about the man who waved at a friend and bought a painting for $5 million are amusing but rarely based on real events.

Some auction goers take delight in bidding on expensive items but are careful not to buy anything: bidding as a public display. Others try to conceal their bids: bidding as a covert maneuver. Some bidders bid often but rarely buy anything: bidding as bottom-feeding. Occasionally, a bidder, as a lifestyle, is unable to come in second in any setting: bidding as personal confrontation. On rare occasions, a bidder is not focused on exactly what they are bidding on or on what they end up buying: bidding as blind entertainment.

One morning at auction school, our guest instructor, an award-winning machinery auctioneer, tall and confident, asked us to pretend we were in a live auction. As he began his melodic chant the students were slow to begin but soon jumped in as the bids climbed to the low thousands. The numbers were very close together and required careful attention to know exactly where the bidding stood.

At one point, a young man wearing a green cap raised his hand to bid $2,800 on an imaginary hydraulic jack for a truck. In an instant, as he began to lower his hand, his bid became $2,900. He jumped to his feet and began waving both his arms. He yelled at the auctioneer, saying that he had not bid $2,900. He was adamant and stayed on his feet, still waving, until the auctioneer finally stopped the auction. The auctioneer, clearly annoyed at being interrupted, pointed at the young man and asked, "You were bidding, weren't you?" his voice an act of authority and condescension.

The young man shouted his response, saying, yes, he was bidding, but he did not bid $2,900.

The auctioneer replied, "After you do this a few years, you will see how it works. You have to learn how to work the crowd." The young man stood his ground, rooted by his anger, a prophet in the wilderness, even as the auctioneer resumed his chant.

As the auction continued with no further discussion, I silently cheered for the young man. This session was intended to demonstrate an example of a flawless chant, but for me, it illustrated the sort of auctioneer I did not wish to be, one who pushed the edges of legitimate bidding. An old country auctioneer once proudly told me he could get three bids off a slow bidder, one when their hand started up, one when it got to the top of its motion, and one on the way down.

I wished for more training sessions in which I heard the words "trust," "values," "accuracy."

The last night of auction school, we tried out our fledging skills at bid-calling. There were thirty-four student auctioneers (two had dropped out) standing in an alphabetical row. I was near the front of the line and decided to sell my three allotted items in a manner closer to what I imagined myself doing later, a style closer to Sotheby's and Christie's auctions, polite, understated, spoken English.

The auctioneer helping the students that night was a tall, friendly gentleman who wore a cowboy hat and boots, a leather sport coat, and a large silver belt buckle; his string tie was anchored by a chunk of turquoise. It was a real auction; there was a room full of people and furniture and household goods to be sold. I was nervous when I stepped up to the podium, as I was not going to reflect the training of the last two weeks.

"Ladies and gentlemen, we are pleased to offer this fine mahogany Chippendale-style chair from the early twentieth century. Who will start the bidding at ten dollars?" I began.

My instructor interrupted, "No, no, let's start over." He was holding a clipboard and started tapping it against the podium to create a rhythm. "I'll start adding words, and you join right in," he encouraged.

"Wanow hunert, hunert, hunert, erdabid, hunert, hunert, say hunert, wanamuh niney, niney, niney, say niney? Erdabid erdabid erdabid, wanamat niney niney nuh niney . . . ?"

His chant was polished, smooth, and effortless, and working down from $100 to $90 was called throwing out the hook, hoping for a bid from an anxious bidder before the bottom was reached. I tried again with my flat words of introduction for the hapless chair, but I was weak and tentative; the chair brought $15.

"Son, I know you're trying hard," my coach said, "but you need to work on your chant. You'll never make it without a good chant. People want to hear it." He was right: this was not the setting for proper English. I switched styles on my second and third items, a wheelbarrow and a portable air compressor.

I summoned my best syncopated lines from the hours of selling cows and utility poles. I plunged in, calling forth the sacred litanies of the auction gods. I sang and barked and thumped the floor with my foot. I kept the numbers, the *nuhs*, the *wanamas*, the *erdabids* rolling like the rapids on a broad, fast river. I gestured. I pointed at people. I clapped. The words, numbers, and connecting syllables spewed out in long, arching spirals. I pointed at the instructor and told him he could ride this train too. I paused only slightly between the wheelbarrow, which sold for $12.50, and the air compressor, which brought $25.00. I wasn't able to achieve a steady cadence, but there were short spans when the torrent of words and sounds created rhythmic patterns.

When I finished, one lady in the third row clapped two or three times. One man took off his cap and fanned the air, a gesture to cool the overheated air. The instructor put his hand on my shoulder and said, grinning through his large, uneven teeth, "Sheeyit, son, where in thee hell did that come from? You hang onto that, you might make it yet."

It was the first and last time I would ever sell items at auction with a chant, well intentioned as my efforts had been. I opted for clarity. The speed and urgency of the chant heard in a livestock or car auction were not a good fit for the auctions I envisioned and often left people hesitant to bid, as they weren't sure where the bidding stood. Was the number the auctioneer repeated over and over the last bid, or was it the bid he was asking for? I hoped my plain words, used thousands of times in the years that followed, would be clear to all present and would identify both the current bid and the next interval.

"The bid is $100. We're asking for $110. Any interest at $110?"

Or, "The lady's bid is $300" (pointing in her direction); "any advance to $325?"

But even now, years after auction school, when I see a herd of cows grazing in a pasture, I sometimes silently mouth a few *nominabids* and sell a couple Black Angus steers.

BANJO

The Dreamland drive-in theater, southeast of downtown Asheville, became a busy, sprawling flea market every Saturday and Sunday morning in the 1970s and '80s. Mack Avery would be there early every Saturday morning, watching people unload in their assigned spaces next to the drive-in speaker stands. He knew which dealers brought the same unsold items every week and which car or truck being unloaded would probably have fresh goods from a basement or attic. Mack excelled at finding the rare and almost rare; on one occasion he bought a small painting for $1 and sold it later for $1,800.

Mack had remarkable reservoirs of unconventional knowledge. He could discuss at length the history of shutter mechanisms on old cameras and name all the tools used by a blacksmith. His knowledge of pottery, textiles, printing, furniture styles, basketry, the history of glass production, and an apparent infinity of other topics served him well in his early Saturday morning foraging. He was also capable of singing Southern Appalachian ballads for six hours without repeating any verse of any song. I had learned this one night years earlier, when we were traveling back from a craft fair in Nashville, Tennessee, pulling a trailer and trying to stay awake.

I went to the Dreamland flea market with Mack a couple times, but I lacked his uncanny skills for finding notable objects. I spent too much time looking at marginal or worthless items and not enough time examining valuable pieces, a critical error.

Most of Mack's finds ended up on the floor of his garage, piles and boxes resting in the order in which they were carried in and leaning against the last load. The air held the suggestion of mold and shellac. A cluttered workbench was visible at one side, usually with a fiddle or banjo in some state of deconstruction, as Mack played and repaired such instruments. He had won several awards for his clawhammer banjo performances.

At the time, I sold the things I found either at the Corner Cupboard Antiques Mall on Wall Street in Asheville or at Franklin's Auction on Gorman Bridge Road. I went to Mack's garage periodically to buy goods to resell. It was always intriguing to see what Mack had found and to swap what we knew or didn't know about unusual pieces: overshot coverlets, left-handed mustache cups, music boxes, bobbin lace, coopers' tools, wooden clock gears, old 78 rpm records of Ma Rainey and Tampa Red.

On one occasion, he had found a fifteenth-century book, and together we explored the meaning of the word "incunabula," the cradle that held the handset type on which early books were printed. Another time, he had discovered a cloth, probably Latin American, used in burials, which led us to investigate the words "pall," which means cloth, and "pallbearer," one who carries the cloth.

Mack, tall and sturdy, was born in Anson County, North Carolina. He often spoke with authority, smiling as he held forth on the obscure details of some arcane relic. He also had a fertile and playful mind. He once asked, during a discussion of the Bible Belt, if there was an Old Testament Belt. He was also, to use a local metaphor, tight as the bark on a tree, so he could not possibly overpay for anything.

Our negotiations over prices lacked the zeal and skill of seasoned traders. Mack would say $15, I would say $5, and we would split the difference. Sometimes, if we were negotiating on an expensive object, say more than $100 in value, we would each write down what we thought the item was worth, and the selling price would be the average of the two numbers. This method required substantial trust, a quality we shared in equal measure. This did not negate polite promotion of our separate viewpoints. Mack would say he had seen a similar basket, the subject of a negotiation, priced in a shop for $18, and I would say yes, and it hadn't sold at that price either. Mack and I often played poker with a group of friends, but when we were negotiating on the price of an item, we left deceit out of the mix. I enjoyed these sessions with Mack, partly because they enabled me to buy merchandise very reasonably.

One afternoon in 1981, Mack and I were working our way through the mounds in his garage when Mack picked up a small print. It was an etching that pictured a seated woman playing a banjo, a child looking over her shoulder.

"I bought the print because I liked the use of a banjo in the composition," Mack mentioned offhandedly, as he handed me the print.

"Is it signed?" I asked. Mack said no, he had not found a signature. I said the print was pleasant enough, but I wouldn't pay the twenty dollars he was asking. We settled on fifteen, and I put it on my pile.

Later, I unloaded what I had purchased from Mack into the old farmhouse on Sugar Creek where I stored my relics. I priced the pieces for my booth at the antiques mall, but I decided to keep the print and propped it up on the wall beside the light switch. A week or two later, the owner of the antiques mall called and asked if I had anything to put in my booth; she said it looked bare and I needed more merchandise. I gathered up eight or ten things, including the print. I remembered I had paid fifteen dollars for it and that it was not signed. I priced it at thirty-four dollars.

Three months later, as I leafed through the magazine *Antiques*, I saw a full-page ad for a print exactly like the one I had put in the mall, the seated woman playing a banjo, a child looking over her shoulder. I was familiar with the details of the image as I had glanced at it every time I switched the lights on or off in the farmhouse. It was offered by a prominent gallery in New York and was obviously quite valuable to merit a full-page color ad. I quickly called the mall and asked if my print of the lady playing the banjo was still there. They said no, it had sold soon after I brought it in.

I felt it all slipping away. I called the gallery in New York and inquired about the print, asking if it was accompanied by any provenance. They said no, all they could offer was that it had been found in North Carolina.

It was almost certainly my print, a third state drypoint etching and aquatint by Mary Cassatt, created in 1893 and titled *The Banjo Lesson*. I asked if it was signed and was told the signature had been found under the original mat. The etching was being offered for $75,000. I can still see the details: the pitch of the woman's tight hair, the white, flat top of the banjo. It was the hidden treasure I wanted so badly to find.

This was the year Jan gave me a box of Mary Cassatt stationery for Christmas.

TRUCK

I held my first auction in late July 1983, having passed the North Carolina Auctioneer Licensing Board exam several months earlier; my license number was NC3041. Mr. Young seated himself on the front row at the extreme left side of the room, a position that made it very difficult for me to see him. He bid by holding his white card in front of his white shirt, and as there was no movement, it was hard for me to tell when he was bidding. About an hour into the auction, after he had bid successfully on a number of items, Mr. Young stood, waving both his arms, and yelled, "You missed my bid. I was bidding on that painting." His face was flushed and twisted, as though his entire body might explode. The orderly, rather solemn texture of the morning splintered, shattering like a pane of glass. People looked around. What was going on? I quickly apologized and kept going, vowing silently to never miss his bid again. I had watched Mr. Young at many auctions and knew he had no fear of embarrassment, nor was he constrained by any sense of social discomfort, but I had never seen a public outburst such as this. Perhaps Mr. Young wanted to make clear to me who was really in charge this morning.

A couple hours later, even with several of the floor workers watching him and signaling to me when he was bidding, I missed his bid again.

This time, he stood up and shouted, "Why don't you look over here? I was bidding on that fender." I was now the object of his wrath. He was not as quaint or amusing as when I watched his antics in his shop. I paused and counseled myself a bit: "Apologize, be polite, don't take it personally, and move on quickly."

But about three hours later, near the end of the auction, probably about the time he was planning to leave anyway, it happened again. He had done nothing all day to make his bids more visible, but he had also bought almost all the expensive lots in the auction. Without his participation, the auction would have been much more difficult.

This time, his fury, real or staged, was not to be appeased. He stood up, waved his auction program in the air, and screamed, "Goddammit, if you're not going to take my bids, you can just keep this stuff," and stormed out of the room. I quickly gathered myself and announced the next lot with a brief description. Upset as I was, I felt a quick breeze of relief and slowly relaxed, now that I didn't have to constantly look his way.

. . . .

On a hot morning the day before the auction, my truck had lurched and rocked up the steep, unpaved road. The last several hundred yards past the end of Sugar Creek Road to our house was slow going in a car but particularly challenging in large vehicles. I carefully maneuvered the big rental truck through the ruts and boulders, briars and bushes scratching the sides of the vehicle. I had stored everything for my first auction in the old farmhouse on our property and was about to load it and transport it to Asheville, twenty miles away. I had rented part of a ballroom at the Inn on the Plaza Hotel in downtown Asheville as the venue for the auction, the preview scheduled to begin at 5:00 p.m.

I was about halfway up our driveway, past the mailbox and on a modest incline, when, inexplicably, the truck stopped. I restarted it, backed up a few feet, and plunged ahead, only to stall again at the same spot. The road was rocky, but there was adequate clearance under the truck. I backed up about fifty feet, accelerated to several thousand rpm, and with tires spitting dirt and rock charged ahead to get past the mystery spot. The truck shuddered and groaned but this time got through whatever had stopped it before. Then I realized the "whatever" was lying across the road in front of and behind the truck: it had caught the power lines, sagging in the heat. I had pulled down five utility poles, and all the lines were now on the ground. Fortunately, there was a crew working on the lines nearby, and despite their justified unhappiness, it took only an hour for the yellow-helmeted linemen to clear the road enough for me to get through to our farmhouse.

It took a couple more hours to load everything, and by the time I backed up to the loading dock at the hotel, it was after one o'clock. I told the first person I saw that I was there to set up the auction preview, advertised to open at five, I added. He said he didn't know anything about an auction and had the afternoon off. The next three hours were a bad dream through which I seemed to move backward; the solution to each problem led to more problems. The tables in the ballroom were full of dirty dishes from an event that morning; the staff who normally set up the room were busy setting up another event; the manager with whom I made the plans was on vacation; and the folding chairs were on buggies in a locked storeroom.

Jan, Andrew, and friends were coming to help set up the preview, but I couldn't wait any longer for help from the hotel. I stacked the dishes and carried them to the kitchen. I cleaned, folded, and rolled away the round tables. I found other stacks of chairs to use and set them up. I positioned the podium, amplifier, and speakers and began unloading the truck.

When my family and friends arrived, I explained how I wanted things set up. I had very specific ideas about all the details: how furniture should be displayed; plans for the arrangement of jewelry and silver in cases; the lighting, stage, and flowers; the music we would play during the preview. I wanted all elements of the auction to be professional and well organized. But I am not by nature a patient person, and situations like this do not bring out my best qualities. I fussed and stewed, anxious about everything. Later, several people even suggested I had been irritable. But by five o'clock, after a frenzied afternoon, the auction preview was set up.

It was important to me that Mr. Young attend the preview and the auction. I had watched him in many auctions he had attended as a buyer; he was rarely outbid. His wife, Ann, and Jerry Israel had arranged to get him to the preview this July evening, and I was relieved when I saw him walk in. He marched up to me and asked abruptly, "Where's the bathroom? You know, bathrooms are very important at an auction." He said that when I got to be his age, I would understand. "You can't have a decent auction without good bathrooms," he instructed as he scurried away.

I tried several times to direct Mr. Young to items I thought he might be interested in bidding on—a bronze replica of Venus de Milo, a tambour desk—but each time, he would nod his head slightly and walk away. He didn't want me or anyone else suggesting what he ought to do. I was relieved to see that he did save a seat for himself for the auction the following day.

The next morning, Jan registered about ninety people, one of many tasks she would be responsible for on auction days for the next twenty-five years. We had advertised the auction in several newspapers and mailed a one-page flyer to people on our recently created mailing list. I had assembled about 450 lots from two small estates, a local appraiser had referred several clients with items to sell, and two dealers had consigned furniture and country collectibles. The auction included a Rembrandt print, pottery, coverlets, jewelry, and a rare copy of *The Crisis in Industry*, the first published work by Thomas Wolfe. Friends from the Southern Highlands Craft Guild had consigned a standard grade Wooton desk.

Regular auction goers found two new amenities: we had prepared a written program describing each of the 450 lots and listed them in the order in which they would be sold, neither done in local auctions. I also thought it would be civilized to take a break midway through the day.

The stage was set. I read the terms of sale, pointed out the fire exits, then introduced our staff of fifteen people: cashier, floor help, and two people to check out purchases against cashier statements. Our clerk, Nancy McFall, was ready to record buyer numbers and selling prices as she would faithfully at our auctions for the next thirty years. I had attended dozens, probably hundreds, of auctions in the past five years and understood the basic dynamics of this process, but I had prepared a few simple techniques to help me keep things moving:

- If I wanted to indicate where the current or winning bidder sat or stood, I would gesture with my right hand but always keep my left hand pointed in the direction of the last bidder, in case I lost track, or vice versa if the current bidder was on my left.
- In auction school, one instructor told us never to say, "I have . . ." when acknowledging a bid. If we said that in an auction exercise, he would shout, "You're not bidding. You don't have nothing." So, I had taught myself to say instead, "The bid is . . ."
- Always go back to the previous bidders, even if they were shaking their head.

Armed with these bits of advice for myself, I plunged in, but soon it all seemed ponderously slow. In later auctions, we would usually sell eighty or ninety lots an hour, but in the first hour or two of this our first effort, we were selling only fifty lots an hour. All the transitions were slow, the first time for everyone in this setting. I also spent far too much time discussing each lot, proudly describing bits of the research I had done. There was no phone bidding and only a few absentee bids, which Jerry executed. Several times during the day, I announced the date of our next auction, about two months later.

I have a photo of Andrew, age fifteen, holding up a Windsor chair in front of the small crowd. Neither he nor I suspected that years later, he would be the head of American Furniture at Christie's New York, make regular appearances as an appraiser on PBS's *Antiques Roadshow*, and eventually become the owner of Brunk Auctions, taking the business to national prominence.

My mood during the auction was not of the "dream come true" variety but closer to "this is work I must do to get this business off the ground." The auction lacked the color and social cohesion of a Friday evening at Franklin's Auction. Few if any stories were told or retold; this auction had no shared history. Most importantly, we offered no stellar objects our buyers *had* to own. No one curled up around their phone on the back row, waiting for their treasure to come up; very few bidders had presented bank letters to ensure that their credit was in place, asking nervously how long it would be until their coveted piece came up. By definition, the dealers had consigned merchandise they had been unable to sell. Many lots sold with only one or two bids, and more than a few passed for lack of a bid. The word "boring" hovers in my mind as I write this. The only moments of drama and suspense were Mr. Young's outbursts.

The printed program was a big hit, as people appreciated knowing when items they were interested in were coming up, but the recess for lunch was a terrible idea. Half the audience never came back after the break. Perhaps these folks were just curious to see what the new auctioneer was up to, he having joined the local posse of over fifteen licensed auctioneers in the Asheville area who sold antiques and related merchandise on a regular basis. After the auction, Jerry and Ann reassured me that indeed, Mr. Young would come by in the morning and pick up his purchases. The auction brought a little over $42,000 but produced no measurable profit.

Despite its shortcomings, I was confident that the pace and the mechanics of the auction would smooth out with time. It was also clear that in the future, we would not take lunch breaks, we needed better things to sell, and Mr. Young would always be welcome.

When the auction was over, as I relaxed in a chair behind the podium, I recalled my hopes that the auction business would lead to a new invention of myself. How was that pretentious plan going after a day of it? Maybe this was just my next big project. Did I want to stand in front of people and talk about money for hours?

I understood this day best when I viewed these proceedings as a cheap variety of theater, everyone holding the script in their hands. This day featured solo performances by two actors, me and Mr. Young, who clearly won the Oscar. My role was to encourage people to spend more money and to help them pretend for a moment that this mattered, that there was a larger purpose underlying this event, something more substantial than whether or not a quilt was worth $140 rather than $130.

If the question was "Can I do this?" the answer was "Yes, I can." But what was the scale of my ambition? Where would this take me? I could not have known that this repeating spectacle would propel me through more than 200 auctions over the next thirty years, or that we would eventually have twenty people on the staff and routinely produce color catalogs.

I also thought back to the beginning of this day, the logistics of setting up the auction, not knowing that in less than two years, we would leave our farm in the country and move to Asheville, depriving me of more auction day adventures that began in a truck, challenging a steep mountain road.

SHINGLE

I figured the whine of the truck tires was about a G below middle C. I have hummed and sung with many appliances and tools over the decades: table saws, tractors, blenders, garbage disposal units—any device with a sustained, audible pitch. The very best are vacuum cleaners with their wheezy, consistent drone. Sometimes I hum with them in a simple harmony, or hold a dissonant note, or sing syncopated fourths and fifths in a medley of sorts. When I stick the end of the hose firmly into a pillow or a sofa, the pitch rises, and I change keys with new improvisation, fabric puckered into the end of the tube.

But on this humid August night in 1985, a serious and more challenging composition lay ahead. I'd left Asheville at 3:00 a.m. and driven a twenty-four-foot rental truck to a small town a few miles north of Tampa, Florida, to pick up a load of nineteenth-century English furniture consigned to one of our auctions. Prior to the eleven-hour trip, I had seen photos of the consignment: desks, chests, heavy mirrors, dining tables, and an oversize Victorian sideboard with a thick marble top. The consignor assured me that a man named Kevin would be at the appointed storage facility near Tampa at 2:00 p.m. to assist with the loading. Yet when I entered the enormous blacktop lot filled with orange-doored storage units baking in the bleaching sun, the staff of one—a woman watching soap operas—said she'd been expecting me but didn't know anything about a man named Kevin.

After an hour of waiting and making phone calls, I finally gave up on my imaginary assistant. I knew it would be a formidable task to load the truck myself, but I hadn't driven eleven hours to turn around and go home empty.

I pulled the truck beside the door to the double unit where the furniture was stored. I had been in many storage units, but there was always a moment of anticipation: Would there be fine things for us to sell, or beat-up reproduction furniture?

When the roll-up door rattled open, the pent-up smell of hot varnish flowed out like a slow sigh. I was pleased to see that the furniture was wrapped in packing blankets and stacked in neat rows. I unwrapped an English butler's chest and found it to be of good quality: inlaid mahogany and original feet and brasses. Good, sellable pieces would make loading them seem more worthwhile. If I tackled each, one at a time, as though it were all I had to load, maybe I could do it.

First, I rolled the chests up the ramp with a hand truck. Next, I disassembled the dining tables and breakfront and maneuvered them onto the truck in pieces. The geometry of the task distracted me from the imposing pile. The most challenging was the thick marble top to the sideboard. I wrestled it onto a blanket on the floor and then slowly dragged it up the ramp into the truck.

Over the next several hours, the inside of the truck grew even warmer than the thick, sulfury Florida air outside the truck. I drank ice water, wrapped a wet cloth around my neck, and tried to work slowly but could not cool down. I was physically fit and experienced in loading trucks, but this task required all my reserves of strength and will.

Even in the earliest years of the auction business, I had sorted through many grimy basements and cluttered libraries and worked with families arguing over the remains of an estate, but this was straightforward grunt work: wrap it, lift it, carry it to the truck, tie it in. I took a short break and looked past the rows of storage units and wondered if they held any valuable objects or just old televisions and mops. For many people, storage units are the institutionalization of indecision. Some pay rental fees for years on a unit full of old textbooks, inherited dishes, and boxes that have been moved many times. Let it go, I want to say, or maybe own fewer things to begin with.

By five o'clock I had finished loading but felt sick. I was shaking and chilled, signs I knew of heat exhaustion. I sat wrapped up in a packing blanket under a small willow oak beside the chain-link fence bordering the storage facility. I drank sips of cold water until I stopped shivering. After half an hour, I was still weak, but it seemed probable I would live. Slowly, I made my way back to the truck and sat in the air-conditioned cab for another half hour.

Despite my fatigue, I could not imagine enduring a lumpy-mattress, stained-rug, stale-smelling, thin-toweled motel room that night. I decided to make the eleven-hour drive home to Asheville. I'm not sure what I was trying to prove; I could afford a nice motel and a quiet meal to give myself some rest. What if it did take another day to get home? Yet it seemed like a waste of time and money to spend my evening just sitting around when I could be driving home. I could hear the voices of my uncles and my Mennonite ancestors, mostly farmers, saying how hard it was for them to sit still when there was work to be done.

The auction business had been the latest reinvention of myself, the most recent in a series of restless investigations of what to do with my life. As always, it seemed, what I lacked in skill and experience I made up for with unqualified resolve. Looking back, I wonder if working too hard was the only organizing principle of my life. Was I trying to prove to the world that I was capable of hard labor? Had I thought about it back then, I might have reasoned that the world wasn't keeping track—that I was the only person for whom proof was required. That logic was not present, however, in the air-conditioned truck cab.

To drive all night, to stay awake and alert, I knew I would need to have before me a challenging task, something to fully occupy my mind. I knew an unreasonably difficult undertaking requiring skill and stamina would keep me interested—something improbable to mimic the drive home. At the time, I sang in a vocal trio with two other men, George Peery and Jeff Stillson, singing mostly early Renaissance music. I wondered, as I sat in the idling truck in the storage facility parking lot, if I could write a composition for the three of us. I decided I would put Samuel Beckett's poem that begins "My way is in the sand flowing / between the shingle and the dune . . ." to music. I imagined three men's voices singing those quiet, introspective words, a cappella. I had recited this poem to myself many times, aloud and silently, since first reading it years earlier. The poem was one of four short pieces Beckett wrote in 1948 while living in Paris with Suzanne Dechevaux-Dumesnil, his partner, five years before writing *Waiting for Godot*, which vaulted him into fame. I wondered if Beckett would have minded an amateur musician putting music to his lines, a translation to three voices. The music would change the color of the words, but so would any interpretative reading, I reasoned.

I had never composed any music but grew up in the Mennonite church singing four-part a cappella hymns. This composition would require three lines of music with no keyboard, no written score, no key signature. I had only the G of the truck tires, the G below middle C, at sixty-four miles an hour, the most speed the yellow rental truck could muster. This would necessitate auditory memory and the ability to imagine how three notes would sound together but hearing them only one at a time. This task was a good fit. I was excited to see if I could do it and exhilarated by the very idea of it.

I filled the truck with fuel, put a supply of cold drinks and food on the seat beside me, and headed north on route 301. Though it was 6:00 p.m., fifteen hours since I'd first left Asheville, I no longer felt fatigue; I was buoyed by the work ahead.

It began this way: I sang the first phrase, "My way is in the sand flowing," eight simple notes within an octave. They came easily, an unplanned line of music. Where did the notes come from? I wondered. They hung in the air for an instant and then were swept away by the roar of the motor and the rattle of the wind against the sides of the truck.

I sang the eight notes over and over, dozens of times, to embed them in my mind, experimenting with many slight variations. One of the eight notes was a G, so I was in unison with the truck tires for one note each time through. They were steady, like a vacuum cleaner. I drove past several lakes, orange groves, and horse farms and then through the town of Ocala, about seventy miles north of where I began. The flat landscape was ablaze with yellow billboards advertising cheap gas, pecans, oranges, and fireworks.

I was ready for what I thought might not be possible: to create a second line of music for the baritone voice against my memory of the first line, the melody sung by the tenor. I tried two notes, then three, and then the entire eight-note baritone line. I sang the tenor line, stopping at each note to sing the baritone note, then sang the baritone part, stopping at each note to sing the tenor note. I was as close as I could get to singing two notes at once. I was afraid to stop, fearful that these imaginary constructs with no weight or history might vanish.

Two hours into my journey, near Starke, Florida, I added the third voice, the bass line, against my memory of the tenor and baritone lines. I sang each of the three lines dozens of times, maybe a hundred times, always anticipating the Gs when I was in tune with the truck tires. I thought about George and Jeff and wondered if we would ever actually sing this thing.

I went to the second phrase, "between the shingle and the dune."

The lines of the poem were familiar to me, but I had never asked the meaning of the word "shingle." A few years earlier, at Pawley's Island, South Carolina, I learned its meaning, and it became a favorite word.

At the beach I rose early one morning to watch the first rays of sunlight, parallel to the surface of the ocean, strike the back of waves, producing shifting pale emerald beams as the light passed through the thin curves at the top of the breaking waves. I paused in my walk to pick up a shell and stood, bent, to examine it. A friendly voice behind me said, "That's called a fractal, you know." It was a man's voice, his words spoken in a slow, low-country cadence, as though we were friends of long standing. I stood and squinted to see him in the bright early sunshine. He wore a weathered pair of oversize shorts, a white shirt, and a sun visor over his white hair. His skin was brown and taut, his bare feet clean and leathery. He was smiling.

"This shell is called a fractal?" I asked.

"No, no," he replied. "That line of sand left by the last wave. The shell you picked up was lying on the fractal."

"I didn't know it had a name," I replied. The rolling edge of water from the last wave made slight eddies around our feet, and we sank very slightly into the sand.

"Oh, yes," he continued, looking out toward the now pink-orange sun. "Everything has a name, and it's important to learn those words, don't you think?" His last three words were joined in a rising inflection: "doan-chew-think?" He asked if I knew the name of the little gravelly section when you first step into the water. He said it felt a little rough under your feet, but it was really made up of small, rounded pebbles. "That's the shingle."

I took five or six steps to the edge of the surf and picked up a handful of the rolling, coarse sand. I poked at the wet mixture of beads of shell— miniature globes and cabochons—spread on my hand and looked up to ask a question, but the man with the meaning of words was walking away, headed north, up the beach. "Thank you," I hollered. He waved one hand, the one nearest the ocean, in forty-five-degree waves but did not turn around. He was quite old and walked with effort, his thin legs swinging in slight arcs as he planted each foot for a step.

After several hours, I began inventing lines of notes for the second phrase of Beckett's poem and then sang through the first two phrases for each part. I did this many times, mile after mile. My euphoria was wearing off as I realized my task had become a geometric progression of complexity: I had eight or nine phrases to go. I was now passing Jacksonville, Florida, in the center of three lanes on I-95. Eighteen-wheelers flew past on both sides, setting my truck rocking from the surge of compressed air. The pavement still carried the heat of the day. I began work on the third phrase.

I thought about Beckett. Had he ever moved furniture in the dead of night? What words would he use to report the experience? When he wrote this poem, he and Suzanne lived a bare, frugal existence, and it seems unlikely that they owned any substantial furniture—maybe a small painting or two. How meaningless it was, I thought, to haul a Victorian sideboard through the August heat, a behemoth few people would want in their home or shop. But I did this because it was my work: I sold things for people, even ungainly pieces I found unattractive. Someone would pay something for it.

The question of why I pushed myself so—why I was unable to rest for a night, why I gripped the steering wheel for eleven hours until my fingers were frozen in stiff coils while the road turned into a streaky blur—that question still goes unanswered. Have I been true to myself? I asked. Or is my life somehow contrived, an artifice, wasted on trivia, lacking coherence and direction? There are never any gaps between projects: I need to always be consumed by my work, to keep despair at bay. The long explosions of personal energy in pursuit of my latest conviction about what to do with my life are familiar to me but rarely examined.

Some days, I make a restless peace with the way I live, allowing myself, for a few moments, to value my choices.

Or perhaps I am trying to leave evidence that I have lived. Minor, incidental traces: a chess set from my days as a woodworker, a stone wall I built on our mountain farm, a bit of music, these words I now write.

Five hours in, the fat bugs of the night made yellow smears on the windshield as the truck lumbered up I-95 through southern Georgia; I was just west of Savannah. There was only the slightest gray in the sky to the west. I was hanging on the steering wheel, holding my body up with both hands. Some of my clothing was still damp, and I realized I was very tired. Eventually, I abandoned the phrase-by-phrase system of learning notes and tried a different tack. I worked on each of the three parts through the entire song. The problems were the same as with the phrase system, however. When I tried to sing against my memory of the other two lines, I repeated notes from the other parts, losing the intricate harmonies I hoped for.

After driving about eight hours, I passed through the sand hills region of South Carolina, an ancient beach and coastline southeast of Columbia that roughly divides the coastal plains and the piedmont. I pictured myself walking along the dunes at the edge of the ocean 20 million years earlier when, in the Miocene era, the beach was formed. That beach was now about 100 miles inland. I tried to imagine 20 million years.

I plodded on with the work, but the distractions grew longer and the lines of music more fragmented. How many hundreds or thousands of times had I repeated these notes? I had more and more trouble finding the G of the tires.

When the truck started up Saluda Mountain at the North Carolina line, I shifted into a lower gear that slowed the truck and created a new, lower pitch from the tires. I lost the G altogether. I had no desire to transpose these lines into another key. It was 4:30 a.m.; the fatigue and monotony were closing in. Fog was swimming past the windshield. The air-conditioned cab felt like an abandoned cave, cold and barren. I had the sour taste of air-conditioning in my mouth. Large green directional signs appeared on the pavement in front of the truck but vanished just before the truck hit them. I was struggling with fragments of the last lines of Beckett's poem: "My peace is there in the receding mist / . . . and live the space of a door / that opens and shuts."

Suddenly, I could not remember any of the words in the poem, none of them. All I could find as I crawled around the debris of my memory were waves crashing on the shore of an ancient beach, mingled with George's clear tenor voice singing his first note, a high G. I stopped singing. I had nothing left.

I gripped the wheel tighter and gave up the song. I did not argue with myself. I focused back and forth between the white lines on the road and the small signs marking tenths of a mile. I was an hour from home.

. . . .

Many years later, long after the all-night truck ride, I explored with my friend Jeffrie the coast of Unst, the northernmost of the Shetland Islands in the North Atlantic. With topographic maps, we searched for small beaches found occasionally along the rocky, imposing shoreline. In these remote places, often between cliffs of red granite, we discovered magnificent shingle beaches.

On one such day, we found a large crescent beach at Burrafirth, past the village of Haroldswick, flanked on both sides by miles of inaccessible, rock-strewn coastline. We parked our car on the thin shoulder of the steep road and hiked down toward the edge of the land. We walked through a large pasture of grazing sheep and then to the water. To the east, our right, we saw an opening in the wall of rock descending from the cliffs above. We walked through it, an archway carved by the ocean, onto an apron of polished stones that spread before us as though one of the giants, who in legend had created the nearby peaks, had spilled an immense bag of jewels. The stones rose from the water's edge and spread to the base of the cliffs. Storms had pushed the piles into asymmetric terraces, some with small pools of clear water.

It was a sunny day in mid-January, and we were dressed against the steady wind, warmed by our excitement. Our only company was the fulmars, perched on small shelves and niches in the vertical walls of stone, gliding in smooth ovals to and from their rough nests, shrieking their protest at our intrusion. We moved with very slow, meandering steps, constantly reaching for yet another remarkable find, as though we had never before seen a stone. Some were perfect eggs, varying from those of a wren to those of an ostrich. We stood frozen in postures of examination until our bodies ached from lack of movement. We were in awe of the infinite shapes and colors. Even the piles of plastic bottles, unraveled blue rope, and other floating trash from ships in the North Atlantic did not distract us. Hours later, when Jeffrie saw the quickly rising tide, she pointed toward the archway through which we had climbed for entrance, and we scrambled over the rounded stones and through the stone-framed passageway.

What would Beckett have made of this immense, mysterious shingle, running up against the cliffs, no sand flowing, no dune? His shingle was probably a short stretch at an ocean's threshold, a couple of steps.

I would like to have walked on these stones with Beckett and asked him.

The scent of the ocean, the beautiful, unfailing wind, the screech of the fulmars, and the glint of ruby, amber, and ivory gave these stones life. I still have a few of them, aligned in a row on a shelf.

....

When I got to Asheville in the truck that August night, I skipped the usual stop at the warehouse to pick up my car and drove directly to our house, the truck tires finally silent. I stood beside the truck for a moment, my hand resting on a front fender, the shoulder of my hardworking old friend. The motor sighed and popped slightly as it cooled. I was the first of our family that morning to stir through the stale, thick air of dog days as I picked up the morning paper and walked toward the door. Condensation dripped off dogwood trees beside our driveway, a slight pink rising in the eastern sky.

I was unable to sleep. Endless loops of memorized notes were ground into my fatigue. I got up hurriedly and made five horizontal lines on a piece of paper, a score of music. Using vertical sticks, I began transcribing the notes of the last twelve hours. They were still there. The words gave them structure.

Several days later, having added measures and time signatures so lyrics and notes were in the proper relationship, I gave my handwritten score to Jeff, a much more accomplished musician than I, and asked if he could find a suitable key for these lines. He looked at the sheet for a while and then asked where it came from. I said only that I was trying to write music for the three of us, using Beckett's lyrics. He looked at the score a bit longer, asked several more questions, and then smiled and said he thought he could "make it work."

I also looked up the meaning of the word "fractal," expecting to find words about lines of sand. Instead, I learned that a fractal is a shape, originally a mathematical construct based on an equation that repeats itself and creates self-similarity. Some mathematic fractals, I read, are generated by repetition of a system of differential equations that individually exhibit chaos. In nature, fractals repeating but not identical shapes are found in snowflakes, lightning, broccoli, blood vessels, and ocean waves, among other venues. The fractals the old man referred to were the lines of sand left by retreating waves, similar but always slightly different: a changing diagram of the ocean's recent history. A series of repeating shapes that, if considered alone, exhibited chaos. Lines of music. A life.

About two weeks later, the next time our trio rehearsed, Jeff produced three clean sheets of music, saying he had written it in five flats. I couldn't imagine writing anything in five flats, but there it was, Beckett's poem put to music for three voices. It had no dynamic markings. George asked how we should sing it, and I said, "Thoughtfully," the only word that came to mind.

I was nervous. I was about to greet a close friend, the music, a friend with whom I had a short but very demanding relationship. I wasn't even sure we were still friends.

We sang through the song slowly, listening for handholds in the melody and harmony. Several times, when the song required obscure intervals or close dissonance, George or Jeff asked, "Is this what you meant?"

"Yes, it is," I replied, the harmonics easily confirmed. The last time we went through the piece that night, I put the music down, shut my eyes, and sang from the front seat of the truck, somewhere on I-26 in South Carolina.

The three of us performed the song once for a group of friends with whom we sang shape note music. About a year after the long truck ride,

Jeff brought me the sheet of music I had originally given him, mounted in a simple wooden frame, the blue ink faded. It is now stored in a box marked "Music, miscellaneous."

It does not matter that the piece is not performed, because I have it in me. When I read the poem, I hear the tune of it, the music moving with and against Beckett's words. I easily imagine the whine of truck tires, the muggy air of that night, holding myself up with the steering wheel. The poem and music are always present when I stand at the edge of an ocean, watching the noisy surge of waves, the silent, changing fractals, the slight rustle of the shingle.

LOG

On a warm, late spring day in 1986, I visited an elderly couple in East Tennessee who had invited me to come and look at their antiques; the caller, a gentleman, said they might want to have an auction. "There's quite a bit to see" he added. I had conducted several auctions in Tennessee and was eager to consider another, as my young business certainly needed more income. I have always felt at home in rural Tennessee: my mother, one of eleven children, had grown up on a small farm just west of Knoxville. I had indelible memories of our family's trips, when I was a boy living in Chicago, to the Knoxville area and the small farm where my mother grew up. I always looked forward to exploring another corner of the region.

As I drove along their gravel lane, I saw two very large cast-iron pots that might have been used to make apple butter in earlier times but were now dense and overflowing with colorful marigolds and zinnias; the oranges, yellows, and reds fused to create what appeared to be a single, immense bloom in each pot. I passed several unpainted sheds and a small barn, and though I had no idea what the buildings held, I always enjoyed the possibility of significant discoveries.

A small brick ranch house rested on several acres of unused pasture, surrounded by rolling fields of recently mown, first-cutting hay. Blue morning glories bloomed on several wooden fence posts. Two people waved to me from the front porch. The man looked to be in his late seventies or early eighties and stood slanted against a porch post. He smiled comfortably beneath his green cap, and as we shook hands, he asked that I just call him Maynard. He gestured toward his wife, saying she liked to be called Dixie.

She wore a white visor and leaned with both hands into an aluminum walker, a small clutch of plastic flowers attached to the frame.

Maynard said they would be happy to show me around, then helped Dixie down the four or five cinder block steps. At the base, she gripped a cane in one hand and hooked her free arm around his right arm and then smiled, saying, "OK, I'm ready." As we slowly made our way toward the buildings, we walked by several old boats perched at slight angles on rusty trailers and a lawn mower protected by an overturned washtub.

We came to a large one-story shed, packed with antique furniture: pie safes, bucket benches, meal bins, spinning wheels, ladder-back chairs— dusty icons of rural life. My eyes skipped around the congestion and quickly counted over sixty pieces of furniture that would do well at auction: a corner cupboard, a sugar chest, spool cabinets, blanket chests, trestle tables. My interest escalated when I saw what appeared to be a fine huntboard, resting under a pile of handmade chairs, the huntboard probably worth $2,000 to $3,000. I didn't mention this, as its value might come in handy in later negotiations.

Maynard and Dixie surveyed their collection more deliberately, pointing to items and retelling the stories of their discoveries. They did this with an air of kindness, as though in the presence of old friends. Dixie pointed at a cider mill and turned toward me. "You know," she said, "we loved looking for old things together. We've been married almost fifty years, and we thought we might open an antique shop someday." She closed her eyes for a moment, perhaps enjoying the memory of that possibility again.

Some pieces had lapsed into the dirt floor; others were missing a drawer or leaned with a broken foot. All rested mute, unashamed, making no claims for themselves, other than having been desired at one time by someone for some reason. Many appeared to have been stored in this shed for a long time. I wondered if this prolonged closeness, like that of a corner cupboard and a china cabinet leaning against each other for years, had resulted in any intimacy. Did the pie safe with rusted tins and the jelly cupboard with traces of old green paint, tight against each other, share their thoughts as the years ticked by? I think they must have at least shared occasional sighs and murmurs.

The barn was stacked with several disassembled log cabins, sorted roughly into stalls, the logs bearing numbers for use in restoration. Dixie rested on a long, squared beam. One small structure, a corncrib, perhaps the jewel of the collection, lay in a cleared center aisle. I saw two short corner logs, one about four feet long, the other eight feet in length, lying on the ground, fitted together, the half-dovetailed joint and hand-hewn surfaces perfectly matched. Even in the dim light, the silvered logs seemed to reflect the sun. I imagined the structure they defined, and saw the one-piece tin roof for the crib leaning against a wall of the barn. Had the Chestnut and Poplar timbers of this crib minded being disassembled, scattered in improvised piles, lacking the precision of their original order? I wondered if they remembered touching each other for all those seasons of rain, summer heat, snow, and ice, their surfaces gradually fitting together more completely.

Maynard showed me a photograph of the crib before it was disassembled, saying that Dixie had helped attach the metal numbers to the logs as the crib was taken apart. Dixie waved a hand in the air and said that they had found the corncrib in a remote section of Tennessee and that to her, it was the prettiest little log crib she had ever seen. I knew how good the photo would look in our brochure advertising the auction. This small, handsome log crib in excellent condition would attract many buyers, including those who would use it indoors in a large store or market. I imagined vigorous bidding.

A chicken coop, tall enough for me to stand inside, was lined with nesting boxes filled with piles and bags of old medicine bottles, carnival glass, pressed glass, and English transferware china. Here, a stack of oyster plates in a failing cardboard box; here, a crate of perfume bottles. Dixie picked up a carnival glass bowl and named some of the most popular colors and patterns, clearly one of her specialties. I recognized the color of her bowl as marigold and its familiar rosy-orange iridescence. Maynard grinned at her and said he had never understood why people paid so much for that ugly stuff. I agreed with him but was careful not to indicate this in any way.

A long cinder block building was crowded with garden tractors, mowers, rototillers, and assorted attachments, most, Maynard said, "needing work." A workbench and a few tools were visible on one side; the air bore the acrid memory of old gasoline. As Maynard surveyed the collection, he pointed silently at part of an old Farmall two-bottom plow. He pointed for himself, not to call it to my attention, and kept his arm steady for a short while, perhaps until he had located the memory of where he had found the plow or where he might find the parts to repair it. Maynard, earlier in his life, may have walked behind a similar plow being pulled by a McCormick Farmall Cub tractor.

I wondered if the rusty plow had memories of its own, like the smell of fresh earth as its then shiny blades slid under the dewy grass on chilly March mornings or the satisfaction of even furrows. Did this old plow dream of a new life as a mailbox support on a picturesque two-lane road or as an ornament in a carefully curated flower garden?

We looked into another long shed, open at one end, full of antique car and buggy parts, wooden steering wheels, windshields, hood ornaments, differentials, stacks of old hubcaps. Here, I thought, might be some especially valuable auction lots. Maynard and I made short forays down several rows while Dixie rested in a chair. When we regrouped near the entrance, Dixie, without looking at Maynard and aware that she now had an audience, said in a loud voice and with a straight face that she had always wondered why people liked this stuff and paid so much for a rusty headlight or a cracked mirror. I admired her carefully arranged irony.

As we slowly worked our way back toward the house, Maynard swung open the doors of the last building, scattering a border of dry leaves. The rambling structure had been added to several times with plywood and minimal framing. Irregular piles of shutters, iron beds, doors, wooden columns, ladders, small sections of wrought iron fencing, and assorted architectural salvage were visible. Everything appeared to be sitting where it hit the ground the day it was unloaded, pushed against earlier finds.

In my mind, our one-day auction had become a two-day auction, possibly with a second auctioneer working with a crew to sell the contents of just this building. It was time to talk, and we headed for the porch. Dixie sat on the seat of her walker, weary from the exertion. Maynard eased himself into a rocking chair and I onto a shaky glider with chipped green paint. A very old black dog lay on the porch, still breathing.

I needed a strong auction, and here was a great assemblage of sellable merchandise. "You sure have some great collections," I began.

I imagined the contents of all the buildings spread over several acres, cars and trucks parked in the distance on auction day. "I don't know how it got to be so much," Dixie said, smiling brightly. She said they just bought things they liked, but it turned out that they liked a lot of things.

Maynard, pleased with his skill and industry, added that he had bought a lot of this stuff to fix up and had sold several pieces after working on them.

"He is right handy, you know," Dixie confirmed, leaning her head toward him a bit.

"Your collections would make a great auction," I declared hopefully. I suggested that instead of moving everything to another location, it would be better to have an auction right here, in the pasture. It would draw a big crowd, and there would be plenty of room to spread things out.

Dixie looked toward Maynard, anticipating what he was about to say. Standing now, his hands in his pockets, he stared at the ground, then slowly surveyed the sheds and buildings. I watched his eyes as they slowly rose to the horizon, where the undulating fields and distant haze merged into the ancient mountains of East Tennessee.

"Well, we have talked a lot about having a sale since we called you, and we just don't think we're ready to do that," he said quietly. "When we do, we're planning to call you. But for now, I think we're going to hang on to things for a while." Dixie looked at him while he spoke; they exchanged quick glances of encouragement.

I realized that their many years of contented marriage, the barn and sheds filled with the objects that had tempted them, and the faintly blue and gray mountains in the distance were all connected. Ownership for them was more complex, and more personal, than the contents of the buildings. Their possessions were deeply secured to their individual and collective sense of self and place.

Neither Dixie nor Maynard had ever mentioned what they had paid for an item, nor had they asked what an item would bring at auction. They had made no efforts to convince me of the merits of any particular piece, or of the entire collection. How much the collection would bring at auction and my commission were often among the first subjects brought up by clients considering an auction. Not today.

Perhaps they imagined the undoing, the disruption, the furniture, tools, old bottles, car parts, and boxes of hardware laid out on tables and on the ground, curious people picking over the piles, pointing out rust and missing parts. I felt their desire for continuity. Just let it be for a while longer, unencumbered. Don't empty the buildings yet.

They understood that eventually things would need to change, but now, here, in this pasture, in the bright sunshine, there was only the certainty of today, their touches and glances, the sweet scent of new-mown hay.

I didn't wish to disturb the truthfulness of this morning or the fine texture of the life they had woven, so I made no further comments about an auction. I looked at the steps up to the porch and at Dixie's walker and imagined a moment of dizziness, a stumble on the steps, or a loss of balance as she shifted her weight; a fall could instantly change their lives. Suddenly,

I wanted to protect them, to shield them from the complexities of aging, to forestall the inevitable, even as I imagined my own decline at some later time, the loss of mobility, dependence.

Perhaps they knew that there was nothing more to dream of, no better expression of what they valued and their affection for each other than this very moment. The collection would no longer grow and would eventually be scattered, diminished by time and circumstance—if not by auction, by other means. The collection would then exist primarily in the stories they could share with each other, but even those accounts, when that was all that was left, would gradually become less detailed, the names of objects and places harder to remember, the eager edges of discovery and joy worn by years of retelling.

Eventually, it would all vanish, even the aspirations of an auctioneer holding a photograph of a small log structure.

We sat on the porch for a long while, silent, enjoying the late spring sun and fragrant air, the steadfast mountains visible to the east.

DOCUMENT

The mountains of Western North Carolina were at their colorful best on this fall morning in 1987. A line of thirty or forty people stood at the entrance to the Asheville Civic Center. They would each pay ten dollars for an informal evaluation of the object they held, a fundraiser sponsored by a local service club. The participants waited with their paintings, porcelain figurines, old books, charm bracelets, carnival glass, odd chairs, and brass candlesticks, all of them hoping for a startling surprise such as they had seen on *Antiques Roadshow*: the old copper lamp that turned out to be a rare Arts and Crafts survival worth $20,000. I was one of three appraisers who annually donated their time to this popular event. I was always hopeful that I would see some outstanding object and be able to offer good news to an anxious participant.

After the doors opened, people were seated in the civic center in rows of folding chairs, waiting their turn to have their pieces examined. Bits of conversation and loud footsteps echoed in the interior of the large arena. One woman and a young girl, who had sat patiently for half an hour, came to my table when it was their turn.

The woman's unnaturally black hair fell in long, uncombed swirls to her shoulders. She stood almost six feet tall, but her stooped posture suggested personal loss and hardship. Her mouth formed a tight, asymmetrical line. Pressed against her chest, she held what appeared to be a handwritten document, rolled in a layer of clear plastic.

She slowly unrolled the document and the plastic onto my table, then positioned four small stones she had brought with her to hold down the corners. She took from her worn fabric purse a recent newspaper article, which she unfolded and placed on the plastic covering the document. The girl stood beside her, watching silently.

Finally, she sat down, looked at me cautiously, took a deep breath, and said in a trembling voice, "I have a copy of the Declaration of Independence. I found it behind an old portrait when I took the frame apart. The newspaper article is about the one they found in England a few weeks ago and how much it's worth."

In some recess of her mind, she may have realized that this piece of paper was not an original copy of the Declaration of Independence. Perhaps she had allowed herself to imagine how her life would change if it were authentic. Maybe she had already made the many decisions this sudden wealth would require; the money was spent. She had brought the document in to confirm what she dreaded, the certain end of her fragile hope, perhaps for a way out of a life she otherwise could not change. I saw immediately that it was a modern copy: the familiar curled and artificially browned edges, the dots of an offset print, a tiny line of text at the bottom with the name of the insurance company who had given these copies away. Nonetheless, to validate her presence and her labors, I examined it carefully.

....

I remembered some of my first days of collecting, years earlier: the boxes I took home from Franklin's Auction on Friday nights and from flea markets, yard sales, and thrift stores, the valuable treasure I imagined might be hidden in each hopeful purchase. I, too, had dreams of sudden wealth: the diamond hidden in a box of costume jewelry, the rare 1873-S Morgan silver dollar, a signed first edition of Thomas Wolfe's *Look Homeward, Angel*.

I thought I was savvy enough not to be seduced into unfounded hopes of discovering something of great wealth, but the possibility of this, however slight, was always with me, a tiny pilot light burning in the crevices of my imagination.

Now I was responsible for explaining the monetary value of objects to others. These events were often an exercise in politeness, finding creative and positive ways of telling people that what they secretly believed to be valuable was actually worthless, or very close to it—a graveyard for private dreams.

Some dreams are based on fragments of information, often originating in family lore. Several weeks earlier, a man had brought into our auction facility a pocket watch that had passed through his family for several generations. He said that he had always been told the watch belonged to Benjamin

Franklin, as it bore his initials, BF, on the back. I saw quickly that the watch had been made in the late nineteenth century, far too late to have swelled the pocket of the famous founding father.

The idea might have originated when a distant ancestor wondered in jest if maybe BF stood for Benjamin Franklin and each relative who repeated the fiction for the next hundred years embellished that possibility a bit, the attribution becoming a certain fact after so many colorful variations of the story had been offered. Or perhaps the watch bearer was not interested in its monetary value but rather the opportunities it presented to repeat its imaginary biography and its implied brush with fame, which brought him a slight moment of joy with each telling.

The woman with the Declaration of Independence and I never had a conversation. After I'd finished examining the document, it became clear by the way in which she asked the question that she knew the answer. "It's not, is it?" she asked. I shook my head slightly. I had no words to offer.

We both sat for a few minutes, sharing the comfortable silence between us, retreating into our thoughts. Her fears slowly turned to calm, her body relaxing as she breathed more easily. She carefully rolled up her Declaration of Independence and tucked it under her arm, now free of the burdens this piece of paper had created.

She took the girl by the hand and walked into the bright air outside the Civic Center.

SPOON

At the start of 1988, Brunk Auctions was still a one-person business. I hired people for auctions and other part-time tasks, but otherwise I met the clients; wrote the auction programs, contracts, and consignments agreements; loaded and unloaded trucks; and conducted most of the auctions myself. One day in May of that year, I was restacking piles of heavy rugs in a shop I was liquidating when a store employee introduced herself as Robin and offered to help. I thanked her for her offer but declined, as there were hours of heavy work ahead. When she offered a second time, I thanks her for her kindness but again turned her down. The third time she volunteered, I relented. By the end of the day, during which she had worked at least as hard as I had without complaint, I offered her a job. She accepted. An interest in silver led her to a careful and ongoing study of the subject, and eventually Robin Rice became our silver specialist, a role at which she still excels, thirty-four years later. She also became our computer specialist and now is vice president, operations manager of Brunk Auctions.

About six months after I hired Robin, a woman brought in a large box of pitted and dented silver plate: pitchers, entrée dishes, bowls, and goblets. Robin went through the box patiently, explaining that there was very little market for modern plated wares. But in the bottom of the gritty, misshapen box, she found two small spoons, each five and a quarter inches long. They were American coin silver and bore the mark of the maker, perhaps the most famous of all American silversmiths, Paul Revere. Robin wrote the following description for the auction program:

Two American coin silver spoons, tapered handles with engraved borders, baroque scrolled cartouche tips, engraved crests with leaping dolphins, maker's mark on back of each lower stem, mark for Revere (Paul Revere II, Boston. 1735–1810). Each 5¼ in. Light scratches and dents in bowls.

We sold the spoons for $19,800. The happy buyer remarked that earlier she had given one of her three daughters a Paul Revere spoon and was delighted to be able to give a similar spoon to each of her other two daughters.

The spoon was made in Boston between 1770 and 1780. Later I discovered that the Metropolitan Museum of Art in New York has in its collection a Paul Revere tablespoon measuring eight and five-eighths inches in length that features an engraved dolphin within a cartouche, which the museum identifies as the family crest of the Sargent family of Massachusetts. This information was crucial, as the two spoons we sold also had engraved dolphins.

As often happened, my interest in the spoons continued well past their sale in our auction. On April 16, 2011, Heritage Auctions sold a set of six Paul Revere tablespoons eight and three-quarter inches long. They were monogrammed "DMS," whom Heritage identified as Daniel and Mary Turner Sargent, he a wealthy Boston merchant and good friend of John Quincy Adams, she the subject of a well-known portrait by John Singleton Copley.

Thus, the pair of Revere spoons we sold were likely made for Daniel and Mary Turner Sargent in the years just preceding or just following the moment when a newly formed nation became known as the United States of America.

I found six auction records for Revere teaspoons roughly the size of the pair we sold, ranging from four and a half to six inches in length. They sold between 2009 and 2021 for prices ranging from $6,500 to $14,000. On June 25, 2021, during a Heritage auction in Dallas, Texas, a world record was set for a Paul Revere tablespoon and, for that matter, any other American spoon: $32,500.

Eventually, I realized that my interest in these two small, humble objects—spoons I had photographed, examined with a magnifying glass, and researched, including the auction history of similar spoons—was more than simply their success in our auction. I was trying to get in touch with something else: I wanted to be as close as possible to this event in America's history. Was there any chance Paul Revere himself, not an employee, had made the spoons? That he was bent in his shop making these very spoons the day of the midnight ride. Even a whiff of possibility seems to have driven my interest, souvenirs of that famous night.

Paul Revere's famous midnight ride occurred in April 1775. Perhaps Mr. Revere was making teaspoons that evening when he learned that the British were coming.

TEAPOT

In the early years of the auction business, I worked out of a small, scruffy warehouse on Carolina Lane in downtown Asheville and had no suitable place for clients to bring things in for possible consignment. I often made house calls, only a few of which led to compelling auction candidates, but I always went when invited into someone's home.

On this cold January morning in 1989, I was in Swannanoa, North Carolina, about ten miles east of Asheville. Mr. Coleman was thinning out some of the things in his house and had a tea service he wanted me to "take a look at." After I knocked, it took him a few minutes to get to the front door, as he walked with careful, uneven steps. He wore a striped shirt and dark trousers from an old suit. He invited me in and pulled out a chair for me in his dining room. He then retrieved a teapot from a nearby china cabinet and positioned it on the table in front of me. "Here's the teapot from the set," he said, with no further details.

I asked if I might go over it. He laughed, saying that would be fine. "I don't think you can hurt it, and if you can get anything for the tea service, you can take it along and sell it for me. I don't have any use for it." He spoke softly and breathed his words slowly, with occasional short pauses. I saw immediately that the teapot was a fine silver example made by Georg Jensen, the famous Danish silversmith, and that it was quite valuable. I explained this to Mr. Coleman and said that if all the other pieces were made by Georg Jensen, it would be quite a treasure. I came to life with the prospect of having such a group to offer. My young auction business needed a Georg Jensen silver tea service.

The other pieces were scattered throughout his house, appropriately an Arts and Crafts–style bungalow. Sensing my enthusiasm, Mr. Coleman worked to recall where the other parts of the set might be found and then, in his elderly, easygoing manner, helped me search for them, despite his apparent discomfort when he walked. He was not motivated by the possibility of imagined riches, rather by the challenge of retracing when and why he had stored things. I was the one carried along by the prospect of something valuable to sell.

It became a modest treasure hunt we both enjoyed. Since we didn't know how many parts there were to the set, we hunted in likely places throughout his five-room house. After a relaxed, hour-long search, we were able to reunite all the pieces. We found the coffeepot in a drawer at the bottom of the china cabinet; the waste bowl in the bathroom, holding toothbrushes; the tea strainer in a kitchen drawer with other cooking implements, including graters, measures, and lemon squeezers; the kettle on stand and burner on a shelf near the back door with large vases and planters; the cream pitcher in the kitchen, full of toothpicks, behind a cabinet door; and the sugar bowl on the kitchen table being used, perhaps accidentally, as a sugar bowl. We now had all the matching pieces assembled on the dining room table. Mr. Coleman said quietly that he had inherited the set and that he was "not much of a collector."

We were looking at a Georg Jensen sterling silver coffee and tea service, an exceptional example of early twentieth-century Danish design and craftsmanship. All the hallmarks on the bases of each piece were identical: the name "Georg Jensen" in oval cartouches with beaded borders and the word "Sterling." The dull, uneven gray surfaces of unpolished silver may have led to the idea that these were not valuable, but the clean lines and elegant ebony handles suggested otherwise. It was an unusual group as it included nine pieces rather than the usual six-piece configuration. Mr. Coleman listened agreeably as I examined and explained the details of his tea service, but he asked no questions.

Mr. Coleman was happy to consign the set to our next auction, and as I packed it carefully into several boxes, it occurred to me that this set might have included a matching tray. I asked if there was any chance there was a similar tray anywhere in his house. At first Mr. Coleman shook his head, but then as he walked around several rooms, he pointed to a closet in his bedroom and said he thought there might be a tray somewhere in there. He said I could dig around in there if I liked, but he was too old to get down on the floor. He said, "You're on your own with that pile of shoes," then smiled and waved in the direction of the closet.

A sloping mound of shoes and slippers mingled with umbrellas, misshapen hats, and leather gloves covered the floor of his closet. I had some experience with a pile of my own footwear in a closet but approached his more cautiously, slowly picking up the musty shoes one at a time, as though there might be a small creature hiding in one. On my hands and knees, I removed twenty-five or thirty shoes, the umbrellas, and the gloves and found flat against the back wall the matching silver tray with ebony handles, wrapped in a fitted sheet, as though someone wanted the tray out of sight. Clearly, to Mr. Coleman, not a piece worthy of display. I took the tray to the dining room table where Mr. Coleman rested and explained that with the addition of the tray, the tea set was now much more valuable. He nodded politely.

I added the tray to the consignment agreement and mentioned to Mr. Coleman that his set would be pictured in the brochure for the next auction and that I would send him one when they were available. Toward the end of our conversation, I realized that Mr. Coleman had never asked what his set might bring at auction. So I mentioned that our estimate for the set would be $8,000 to $12,000. He said that would be fine but showed no interest in the numbers. Before I left, Mr. Coleman thanked me for helping him find and identify all the pieces of the tea set.

What a pleasant and rewarding morning it had been, working together to bring the set back to life. I often worked with clients to lower their expectations for the value of an object, especially older clients, who often believed that if something was "very old," it was certainly valuable. But I didn't need to convince Mr. Coleman of anything, and I enjoyed working without the pressure of a client's expectations. He also had not walked around his house holding up other things and asking what each item was worth, a common question with clients in these settings. Mr. Coleman showed no inclination for that sort of drama. Neither did he seem to be interested in the details and history of his tea set. How different from my busy days of research, auction records, provenance, market trends.

The mysteries and satisfactions of my work had barely overlapped Mr. Coleman's quiet life. The only thing connecting us was a teapot. The universe I had created for myself, a world that often seemed essential and vital to me and through which I often hurried with a sense of urgency, was not a realm shared by very many people. On this day, working with Mr. Coleman, it seemed important to consider this. Just as not everyone is interested in learning to identify birds, play chess, fish in remote streams, knit clothing for deserving children, or write computer code, only a relatively small number of people in our culture are interested in the decorative arts. I wondered if the usual definition of decorative arts was too narrow: period furniture, Persian rugs, silver, porcelain, fine paintings, all subjects of scholarly investigation. But some homes are lined with handwoven pot holders, finished cross-stitching kits, inexpensive souvenirs, children's drawings, framed jigsaw puzzles, and photos of cats and dogs arranged in collages, all with oft-repeated stories of origin. Perhaps these decorations are also worthy of serious study.

Later, I learned that Mr. Coleman's tea service set was designed by Johan Rodhe in collaboration with Georg Jensen. This style, known as "Cosmos," had been introduced in 1915. I was pleased to include the set in our next auction and featured a large photograph of it in the black-and-white brochure for our March 18, 1989, auction. It sold for $20,000.

Because they are rare, there are few auction records for nine-piece Cosmos tea sets with the matching oversize tray with ebony handles. But at Sotheby's New York, on April 16, 2019, I found a nine-piece Cosmos tea set and tray, which sold for $22,500, including buyer's premium, a set very similar to the one we sold thirty years earlier for $20,000. If in calculating the value of Cosmos tea sets, one subtracts for a modest rate of inflation, these tea sets, at least Mr. Coleman's example, had decreased in value, contrary to the common assumption that fine and decorative arts increase in value over time.

GOLD

Traditional Mennonites are not attracted to showy gold jewelry and fashionable watches, but my aunt Stella, who died at age 101, was something of an exception. In her late eighties, having outlived some of her teeth, she had a double gold crown replaced. She asked the dentist if she could keep the old crown and had it mounted as a brooch, which she often wore, especially at dressy events. People would ask where she had found the unusual brooch; its rounded contours and asymmetrical form suggested it might be an original work of abstract art or the work of a famous designer. She encouraged such speculation, saying she found the design very pleasing. I don't know if she ever gave the name of her dentist as the designer, but she was certainly capable of such mischief. Eventually, grinning, she would recount the well-worn tale of the brooch's origin.

When I began the auction business, I had little experience with gold in any form, but I was reminded of Aunt Stella when a woman consigned a chunky gold nugget to one of our first auctions. She explained that her grandfather had brought it back from Alaska during the gold rush of the late 1890s. She showed me a box of her grandfather's mementos, where she had found the nugget and its thin gold chain. The box contained mostly faded photos of men, dirty and tired, wearing black hats and holding shovels and picks. I was pleased to offer the nugget in our next auction and mentioned in my remarks that it came from Alaska during the gold rush. It sold for about $300, roughly its value as scrap gold.

About a month later, the woman who bought the nugget contacted me to report her displeasure. She had taken it to a jeweler for a new mounting and was told that it was not gold at all but a hefty lump of brass under a very thin layer of gilding. She wanted her money back. "Of course," I said. I learned several lessons from this experience, including that all unmarked gold must be tested and that all descriptions are suspect unless verified in some way, a lesson I would need to learn over and over again. I was, and still am, attracted to engaging, improbable stories. I wondered about the consignor's grandfather. Had he been fooled, too, or was it a cheap souvenir he knew was a fake and brought home as the basis for colorful storytelling?

A year or two later, after one of our auctions in Asheville, a man came up to me and abruptly said he wanted to talk with me. He was very thin, wore a threadbare shirt, and carried a heavy briefcase in one hand. He did not introduce himself but said he had just found out that he was the executor of the estate of a woman who had recently died, a woman he barely knew. He had seen my name in one of our local auction advertisements and asked if I was a licensed auctioneer. I said yes, I was. He wondered if I would come to her house in Waynesville, thirty miles west of Asheville, to see if there was anything we could sell. He hoped I would find something to make my trip worthwhile and seemed to be nervous about his role as executor, as though he needed to produce something valuable.

I met him several days later on the front porch of an older four-room frame house in a neighborhood with no sidewalks. He opened the door to a dusty, almost barren interior. As we made our way through the rooms, I saw a few faded and worn garments hung in a closet and bowed pantry shelves supporting a few canning jars of peaches and tomatoes, the lids rusted and covered with heavy dust. The executor apologized again for the lack of any valuable pieces for me to examine. The spines of several books were visible in a bookcase: English editions of works by Dostoyevsky and Tolstoy, Russian dictionaries, and guides on how to learn the Russian language, all showing signs of recent use. He explained that at age eighty-six, the woman had decided to learn Russian. He added, prophetically, that she was "somewhat eccentric."

The fifteen-minute tour of the four rooms had disclosed nothing fine, important, or even interesting. As we walked through the house, I occasionally glanced out the windows to see if there was anything of value behind the house, perhaps a cast-iron planter. I kept noticing holes, eight or ten freshly dug cylindrical craters, spaced irregularly throughout the area.

When we ended our tour, standing in the kitchen, I pointed out the window and asked the executor what had happened in the backyard. He explained that when he went through the woman's safe deposit box at the bank, he found a detailed map indicating all the places where she had buried gold coins, including a list of the coins in each hole. She had flopped down boards to make a path for her wheelchair; then, from a sitting position, she had dug shafts with a shortened posthole digger and dropped the coins into the holes. He said that the map proved to be very accurate; he had excavated every location and found all the listed gold coins. He added that her will further directed that the coins be sold and the proceeds donated to the American Communist Party.

With that, he set his briefcase on the kitchen table and pulled out a cloth bag, from which he emptied clear plastic bags, one bag for each hole, each holding a few gold coins, a total of about forty. I looked at several and saw that they were in good condition.

The executor asked if they were worth anything. He said he knew nothing about gold and thought the woman who had lived here was "way off in her head." He assumed she had buried worthless coins, play money or tourist souvenirs. I assured him that they were indeed gold coins and added, to his obvious relief, that we would be happy to sell them in an upcoming auction.

We offered them several weeks later, the proceeds totaling close to $11,000. I followed the instructions in the will carefully, though I don't recall how I located the American Communist Party.

I wondered about this convergence of unlikely events: a strange executor whose name I didn't learn until he signed the consignment agreement, a deceased woman with peculiar fixations, a shortened posthole digger, Dostoyevsky, the American Communist Party. I was reassured by a bit of normalcy when the check for the proceeds was cashed.

....

Several years later, in 1996, we were asked to consider selling a collection of coins in the estate of a doctor who had lived in Wilmington, North Carolina. The executor of the estate, an attorney, invited me to Wilmington to examine the collection. Several days later, I drove up to an expanded version of a three-bedroom brick ranch in a 1950s subdivision in Wilmington.

All the personal property in the estate had been dealt with, and the house was empty except for the mildewy coin room in the basement. I saw stacks of back issues of *Coin World* and other periodicals, bound price guides with many yellowed paper bookmarks, boxes of unused coin holders, and bags of coins perhaps waiting to be sorted.

The attorney said the owner had collected coins all his life and that in his last years he had lived alone. I easily imagined him spending unbroken hours and days, carefully examining his coins and adding new purchases. A large coin collection offers infinite opportunities for sorting, grading, labeling, looking up values, buying new coins, and researching the history of a particular date or denomination—not unlike assembling a thousand items for an auction and writing careful descriptions for each.

Filing cabinets and shelves were stacked with rows of narrow coin boxes, filled with coin holders and coins, most with handwritten notes: the year, mintmark, grade, value of the coin, and date of purchase. After an hour of quickly opening and closing drawers and heavy boxes, I agreed to sell the collection. There was plenty here for a good auction. Eventually, we would learn that the collection included over 50,000 coins, not counting the four bags of loose coins.

A few days later, I returned with my friend and coworker Fulton and a small truck, loaded the coins, and carried them back to our office and auction gallery, at that time located in the Haywood Park Trade Mart in downtown Asheville. Fulton, a former helicopter pilot in Vietnam, strong of body and spirit, cook, problem solver, truck and machinery driver, licensed auctioneer, engineer, and security specialist, had recently joined our staff. He became an essential part of our work and an enduring friend. On many drives home, returning from work in a distant place, we offered to each other our differing solutions to the major social and political issues of the day, helping diminish the tedium of long truck rides through the gloomy and sometimes rainy nights.

After Fulton and I had unloaded all the coins, I set up my workspace in a back room, out of sight from exterior doors and equipped with our safe, tables, good lighting, magnifying glasses, reference works, and recent price guides. I sat for a moment and surveyed the mounds of boxes on the sagging tables and the floor, the coins weighing hundreds or perhaps even a thousand pounds. Could I possibly do what I had told the executor I would do, examine, sort, and catalog 50,000 coins? I smiled. I had invented another challenging task for myself and was eager to begin.

The next morning, I made a preliminary survey of the collection and met the solemn faces of famous Americans, mostly men, Susan B. Anthony the only exception, staring out of the clear plastic windows of the coin holders: George Washington, Benjamin Franklin, Native Americans, Franklin Delano Roosevelt, Abraham Lincoln, Thomas Jefferson, and others. None were smiling; all seemed caught in some moment of boredom, indifferent to the thousands of young and old collectors who, for many years, in some cases over a hundred years, would stare back at them for long minutes, examining the wear to their hair, nose, or chin or wondering about the spiky hair (actually a crown) of the Peace silver dollar. Only John F. Kennedy seemed to have a slight smile. I was also reacquainted with the iconography of national symbols: Independence Hall, Monticello, the Liberty Bell, the Lincoln Memorial; Lady Liberty seated, standing, and walking; eagles and stars, shields, wreaths, wheat, fasces, torches, buffalos. I enjoyed the currents of American history threaded through the stacks of coins.

I began with Mercury dimes; there were over 5,500 of them organized only by type, not by date or value, except for rare dates, which were usually grouped. Like many children, I had collected coins, working hard to fill the familiar folding blue binders. Unlike silver dollars, Mercury dimes (actually Liberty with wings rather than Mercury) were accessible to me. I would go to the bank with two ten-dollar bills, borrowed from my father, and trade them for rolls of Mercury dimes, which I would look through, searching for scarce dates, and then return to the bank to exchange for new rolls. My father always reminded me to return his two ten-dollar bills.

Now in Wilmington, I was fifty-four years old, but the awe with which I had held the 1916-D as a boy was still a graphic memory. I often stared at the space for it in the binder, filled with a circular plug on which was printed "Rare." This signified to me that I would never find one. I also recalled the smell of used silver coins, faintly metallic but warmer, smoother, and carrying the collective scent of the thousands of hands, pockets, and purses that had held them and the pay telephones through which they had dropped. As I now worked my way through the Wilmington collection, I passed hundreds of common dates, and then suddenly I was holding five of the rare 1916-D dimes in my hand.

I was quickly seduced by the hunt for rare coins, as I remembered most of the scarce dates and mintmarks. In the following days and weeks, I found the most famous Lincoln head cent, the 1909-S VDB (there were six), the 1914-D Lincoln head cent (there were two), the 1932-D and 1932-S Washington head quarters (there were three of each), and even a 1918-D eight-over-seven Buffalo nickel.

I worked my way through approximately 4,000 Washington head quarters, 2,300 Buffalo nickels, 1,400 Walking Liberty half dollars, 300 large cents, colonial coins, 2,100 Indian head cents, bust-type Liberty Seated dimes and quarters, 18,000 Lincoln head cents, silver dollars, half dimes, gold nuggets, silver ingots, commemorative silver, advertising and souvenir coins, and over 200 US proof sets.

The nineteenth-century silver coins were a revelation; I learned the importance of surface in old coins. Novice collectors often polish old coins to make them shiny, not realizing that the coins get shiny because surface is removed. For some collectors, the most highly sought-after coins are those that have never been touched and have a frosty blue or rich, iridescent blue-purple patina. Copper coins will develop variations of deep magenta and chocolate. The surfaces of these coins are delicate, rare, and, to those who collect them, works of art, something I had never considered. Occasionally, I would find a Barber head quarter or half dollar with these luminous colors and marvel at their survival.

As I wrote the descriptions, grades, and condition of every lot in the auction, I thought of generations of Mennonite farmers who had preceded me. These sturdy men in their overalls, hats, and sunburned faces enjoyed an enduring reputation for being honest and trustworthy. I wanted my efforts to write accurate, careful descriptions to be a direct descendant of that tradition.

As I sorted and cataloged, I often thought of the owner, the man who had assembled this treasury of coins. I came to trust his careful, thorough notes, as his grading standards for the coins were slightly conservative, almost identical to my grading criteria for the auction program. I wondered if he thought about the final disposition of his collection or the person who would examine his notes and study his findings. I imagined us becoming good friends, discussing coins, trading childhood stories of discovery.

I did wonder, though, why he had amassed so many coins of little or no value. Many of marginal value were grouped into large lots for the auction; "about 3,600 assorted wheat pennies, mixed dates and grades," the catalog would read. But if you subtracted 3,600 wheat pennies and another generous 1,000 for scarce or rare pennies from the 18,000 Lincoln head cents, there were still 13,400 pennies left. Why not take 10,000 of them to the bank and come home with a crisp $100 bill?

Perhaps the coins were his friends, the substance of his life, offering the breath of companionship. They required nothing of him but provided him with unending opportunities for study, spreading out before him like a small continent, their tiny mysteries always available to him. Did he speak to them when he found a unique detail? Maybe he could not imagine his life without them, though at the end of his life, he may not have known they were there. We would examine his collection with respect, I mused, but eventually it would be converted into one piece of paper with a number printed on it.

It took several months to finish my work with the coins. I worried that some of the rare coins were fakes, made by adding or subtracting elements to and from the surface. For these, I sought the opinion of experts, coin dealers I knew and respected who were familiar with the many forgeries. In their opinion, none of the coins they examined had been tampered with.

The four bags of coins turned out to be of no numismatic value; many were very worn, lacking readable dates, and some were clad silver coins of no importance. I cataloged the four bags as one lot, the estimate $400–$800.

The 100 gold coins were among the most valuable in the collection and combined all the elements of desirability: scarcity, high grades, intrinsic value, and in a few cases exceptional color, shades of iridescent rose and orange.

When we advertised the auction of the collection, dealers and collectors soon made appointments to examine the coins. Most were men, many wearing long-sleeved checkered shirts and carrying briefcases, lighting devices, folding magnifiers over their glasses, and a recent issue of *Coin World*—caricatures of themselves. They were engineers, dentists, electricians, architects, scrap metal speculators, and coin and stamp dealers; one was a Presbyterian minister. Some were aesthetes interested only in beautiful coins—the Saint-Gaudens twenty-dollar gold piece or the Walking Liberty half dollar, not the bland V nickels.

They sat for hours, some for several days, examining the coins, noting defects, checking grades, and calculating what they would bid for each lot, an infinity of details. "Who graded these coins?" some asked.

"I did," I would reply.

"Did you look at all of them?"

"Yes, I did, in one way or another." A few asked if I guaranteed the grades.

"No, we don't," I replied. "The grades are our conservative opinions. If your opinion differs, you should bid accordingly." I referred them to our terms of sale, which read, "If you require absolute certainty in all areas of authenticity, we recommend you not bid on the item. You should make your most careful examination before you buy, not after."

The coin auction began at four on a Saturday afternoon, having been preceded by a full day of decorative arts, furniture, paintings, rugs, porcelains, and other collectibles. About a hundred people had assembled for the second session of the day. Most seemed to take this event very seriously and sat mute, unsmiling, almost grim, patients waiting for dental appointments.

The auction moved along quickly; we were selling about a hundred lots an hour, one every thirty-six seconds. About half an hour in, we came to the first group of gold coins, beginning with a US 1897-S five-dollar gold coin, the grade AU, almost uncirculated. The bidding rose quickly to $550. About halfway to that price, a man sitting in the extreme back left corner of the room entered the bidding. He was middle-aged and wore thick black glasses and a black leather jacket too large for his small shoulders. He held nothing in his hands—not our printed program, no book of coin values. He bought the first gold coin and the next two or three. It was soon clear that it was going to be difficult to outbid him for any gold coins, whether they went for $200 or for $3,000. The bidders who had spent so much time calculating what a fair price would be for each lot got restless; all their figuring didn't seem to matter.

As more gold coins came up, there was visible and audible frustration. Whenever he bought another gold coin, several people would swivel around and glare at him, muttering their displeasure. He paid no attention to them, just waited for the next one. He spoke to no one and never left his chair.

Several frustrated bidders huddled together, planning to dethrone him by outbidding him on several lots, sharing the cost, whatever it took, figuring if they could break his grip on the gold coins, they would at last be able to buy a few coins themselves. Their efforts failed. They took turns chasing him, but he could not be outbid. His bidding style became an excellent strategy. As bidders gradually tired of chasing him, the prices for gold coins slowly became more reasonable.

What made them particularly angry was that the accepted values for the coins, the structure upon which their collections or transactions rested, were irrelevant. The man in the black coat had a different business plan.

Then, I got worried. I realized I didn't know this man, I had not seen him during all the hours and days of preview, and he was spending a great deal of money. He showed none of the usual concerns over high prices, the slowing decisions, the anxious looks at price guides. What if he was crazy and not planning to pay for anything? I had Fulton take over the podium so I could find out what was going on.

I went to the registration desk and asked Jan what sort of credit arrangements he had made. He had produced a driver's license and two credit cards but not a bank letter of credit, which we liked to see. It wasn't a matter of him running off with the coins; he would not be given his coins until the money was safely in our bank. The problem would be if we ended up with all the gold coins again and had to recreate the auction later, a very difficult proposition.

I decided to speak with him. Kneeling beside him, making as little stir as possible, I whispered, "Sir, you are spending a great deal of money, and I need reassurance that you plan to pay for your purchases."

He turned to me, smiled slightly, and waved a hand in my direction as if to shoo me away. "Don't bother me. I don't want to miss anything. Don't worry about the money." I realized that with no auction program in hand, he was listening for the word "gold," a signal that a gold coin was up for sale.

He bought all the gold coins and several other rare pieces, about 70 percent of the total proceeds for the auction, and paid by wire transfer several days later. After the auction, I was told by someone who seemed to know him quite well that the man was from New York and knew very little about gold coins. He had a tiny gallery in Manhattan where he sold single US gold coins, mounted in small, very fine gilt frames, to wealthy tourists who also knew very little about US gold coins. They were priced at two or three times what he had paid for them, whatever that number happened to be.

His audacity reminded me of my aunt Stella; gold apparently inspires such confidence.

SILENCE

Benefit auctions seem like an easy formula: gather up donated works of art and craft, gift certificates from restaurants and merchants, weekend excursions to the beach or a mountain cabin, and then sell it all at auction to raise money for a worthy nonprofit organization. Brunk Auctions has conducted over fifty such events, but I was often reminded of a continuing education session I attended soon after I became an auctioneer. The featured speaker, an auctioneer with twenty-five years' experience, cautioned that benefit auctions were the most difficult work auctioneers were asked to do: selling the unwanted, to the unwilling, with the untrained.

In one of my first benefit auctions in 1984, a well-known musician was critically ill, and his family needed money for unexpected medical expenses. An informal group of friends and supporters put together a benefit auction to raise money. Donations were gathered and volunteers recruited to help with the auction. Items were laid out on eight-foot folding tables: a set of golf clubs, a voucher for a free dental exam, a twenty-dollar gift certificate to Hardee's, a used NordicTrack exercise machine, four piano lessons, glass ornaments featuring rabbits and birds, an encyclopedia set, a car stereo system, and a bowling ball, among many other items. The lot numbers were written on sticky notes. I was one of several auctioneers who had volunteered to help.

In a friendly voice, the volunteer responsible for registering over a hundred people asked each person which number they would like for their bid cards, not understanding the linkage between the buyer's number on the cards she was passing out and the cashier statement that would list what each buyer had bought: the items they would be given when they checked out. She issued two number sevens, three number elevens, and two number twenty-ones, presumably references to gambling odds.

When the auction was over and the participants had paid for their purchases, the confusion at the checkout table where people were to collect what they bought did not reflect a spirit of brotherly love. Several fierce arguments erupted in which multiple people claimed to have bought the same item. No reasonable way to settle such conflicts seemed to be available.

At another event several years later, a volunteer was holding a large handcrafted bowl that featured a rich red glaze with streaks of blue. It was the third item of about seventy in the auction to benefit a museum. The modern, reduction-fired stoneware was heavy, and the volunteer's movements were uncertain as she rotated the bowl from side to side. She seemed to be self-conscious in front of people, perhaps not comfortable with herself as part of a display. As she tried to show the back of the bowl, it fell from her hands. When it hit the uncarpeted floor, it exploded, the tension fired into the body of the great bowl released into space. Red and blue shards ricocheted off chair legs, some skipped like round stones on flat water, and a few reached a wall sixty feet away. People gasped and shrieked, inhaling and exhaling sounds of dismay. Two staff members came to comfort the distraught volunteer and stab at the pieces with a plastic broom.

When the shock of the moment had passed, I searched for words to ease the pain. I urged people to understand that this was an accident and no one had been hurt; it was not a life or a relationship. We could ask the potter who had donated it if he could make a replacement bowl.

I strained for an hour and a half to heal the fractured air, but the bowl's crash had changed the mood of the evening. People were distracted, still talking about the bowl, glancing around the room. Several lots were passed for lack of bids. The volunteer had been trying to be helpful, but someone more familiar with handling fine objects—say, a staff member of the museum—might have been a better choice.

One of the most enduring fictions believed by planning committees for these events is that lots of alcohol leads to a looser crowd and higher bids. At one such event, sponsored by an artists' guild, a man seated in the back row and wearing a hat with a small feather bid on almost every painting that came up. He kept his paddle high, pausing occasionally to have another sip of bourbon from his pocket flask. He bought the first six or eight paintings and continued to buy several others. After winning the tenth painting, he stood, a fierce grin on his ruddy face, and announced in a loud, unhappy voice, "I actually don't want any of these paintings. I think most of them are really ugly. I'm just trying to help y'all out a little bit."

Later, in the mid-1990s, I was asked to conduct a benefit auction for a large nonprofit agency. It was held in the lavishly decorated ballroom of a country club. The theme was outer space: the ceiling was draped in black fabric, speckled with small lights to imitate faraway planets and stars. Music from the movie *2001: A Space Odyssey* gave the room a convincing ambience. The decorations were intended to suggest total darkness, with only minimal lights glowing at each table. Many people had worked long hours to create the solar system murals and photos of constellations in the night sky; tiny strobe lights imitated falling stars and meteors.

When I was introduced as the guest auctioneer, however, it was quickly apparent that we could not conduct an auction in the dark, but if we turned on the lights, most of the illusions of outer space would be diminished, as if a sudden dawn were breaking in the sky. Much to the chagrin of those who had worked to decorate the room, the lights were eventually turned on, and as with dawn, all the planets, falling stars, and meteors disappeared.

At another event, in order to attract patrons of all interests and persuasions, a museum auction committee in South Carolina had planned multiple attractions: stations with gourmet food, a scavenger hunt, three open bars to encourage revelry, and a silent auction, all in addition to a live auction, which I had been asked to conduct. When I arrived at the auction venue a short while before it began, very few people were seated for the event, and almost all were women. Then a breathless voice on the public address system announced the schedule: in ten minutes, the live auction was to begin on the second floor, and live belly dancing would begin on the first floor.

....

Early in 2001, I was invited to be the guest auctioneer and co-master of ceremonies at a well-publicized benefit auction. A local television celebrity and I were to host the event. The agency hosted an annual gala, the previous year's being a 1920s-style dance with a live band. This year, it was to be a bachelor auction, a popular format for raising money at the time. The black-tie event would include a catered sit-down dinner and cash bar prior to the auction.

Several months before the benefit, I met with the planning committee. The agency director introduced me to the committee, assembled in a conference room. The chairwoman of the program committee, hoping for a total of thirty bachelors, listed the men already committed to the event. The chairwoman of the decorating committee spoke about the stage, lighting, flowers, and dating motifs to be at each table. A well-known jazz trio would play as people entered. Other members described publicity, tickets, money collection, and budgets. It was a festive group, excited about a format they felt was more promising than previous galas.

They asked me what I thought, clearly hoping for affirmation of their work. I said it looked like a good plan and mentioned they needed to ensure the auction itself went smoothly, including registration, clerking, money collection, sales tax if applicable, and checkout. I discussed some of the chaos and memorable failures I had witnessed in previous benefit auctions and emphasized that this format had risks; it was crucial that there be planned bidding for each bachelor so awkward moments would be avoided. I was assured there would be three or four bidders ready for each bachelor.

We had one later conference call prior to the event to make sure everything was proceeding as planned.

Over 250 people attended the event in the civic center, guests paying $200 per couple. Many businesses and supporters sponsored tables for the dinner. The air was charged with expectation: women in skimpy cocktail dresses, a drink in one hand and a program in the other, cheering and squealing as the bachelors, in variously colored tuxedoes, red roses pinned to their lapels, walked across the stage before the bidding began. One bachelor wore cowboy boots with shiny silver spangles. When the auction began, people had been eating and drinking for two hours.

My cohost, a confident woman, comfortable in front of people, introduced each bachelor, noting his profession, hobbies, food preferences, and idea of a romantic evening. Several introductions included vague innuendo: "He likes everything hot!" "Be ready for a complete evening."

A favorite piece of music, chosen by each bachelor, was played while he was introduced. Bidding was spirited, many women shouting out their bids with smiles and laughter. Most bachelors brought between $800 and $1,500 but several brought more than $2,000, one a well-known former college basketball player, another a popular DJ from a local radio station. Each successful bidder was awarded an evening with her bachelor; dinner and dancing were to be part of each date. As each bachelor was sold, the winning bidder came to the stage, kissed her bachelor, and walked off hand in hand with her prize.

Toward the end of the evening, bachelor number eighteen, of twenty-five to be auctioned, walked to the stage accompanied by a jazz version of "Wade in the Water." He was strikingly handsome and wore a pale lavender tux. I thought of the male models wearing sport coats in fine men's clothing catalogs. He was an accountant, a runner, liked Italian food and quiet walks along the beach. He described himself as trustworthy and loyal. And he was Black.

There was no stirring in the crowd, no women running to the front of the stage during the introduction. I asked for an opening bid of $500. Nothing happened. As the excited conversation accompanying the exit of the last bachelor and his date subsided, silence spread through the civic center. I was seized by ominous fear as I asked again for an opening bid of $500. Again, there was no response of any kind. No one moved, and none wanted to look—a scene of inconceivable social nakedness.

In my best upbeat voice, I asked the cohost to run through the profile again for this bachelor and for the music to be played again, assuming the agency director and the committee members would quickly respond with bidders to avoid any further embarrassment. The man stood stoically, his smile now slight and forced.

"Now," I asked, "who will start the bidding at $300?" I was greeted with a silence as long and cold as a glacier. Not a word was uttered, nor was there the slightest movement of any hand. The low murmur of conversation and the slight rattle of dishes ended. I asked again and realized I had no alternatives. How could I end this? The bachelor and I looked at each other, a flicker of acknowledgment that we were both trapped. It was a surreal loneliness, he and I standing on a stage with spotlights on us, paralyzed. There were no glib words, no humorous anecdotes to recall, nothing to which people's attention could be diverted. There was nothing but malignant stillness.

Finally, I made a sweeping gesture with my hand and declared, "Sold, $300 to number 135," the number of a bid card I could see lying on the table where the agency director was seated. The bachelor left the stage, unescorted.

I wanted to go with him and walk beside an ocean somewhere, listening to the quiet rhythms of the waves.

CHEST

The twelve-room nineteenth-century house had been the family's flagship home in Johnson City, Tennessee, for several generations. We had been asked by one of the heirs of the estate, Mrs. Sawyer, to go through the rambling three-story steamship Victorian house to see if there was anything suitable for one of our auctions. Fulton and I were accompanied by Robert, a graduate of Mars Hill College and a dependable employee for several years. We worked our way through musty rooms and a confusing tangle of hallways and pushed open eight-foot oak doors that carried the scent of old varnish. The house was empty except for things too heavy or difficult to move: a rosewood piano, oversize brass sconces attached to the walls in the entryway, large cast-iron pots in the basement.

On this cloudy summer day in 1989, we met with Mrs. Sawyer, a pleasant woman in her fifties, who explained that there were two other heirs, her siblings. She asked if we could sell the piano. I replied that despite the extensive use of rosewood veneer, there was very little market for these Victorian pianos, often called square grands, despite their being rectangular in shape. They were heavy, difficult to move, and, to some people, unattractive. I explained that although they were a fixture in many fine nineteenth-century parlors, most people now preferred a small baby grand that would stay in tune more easily and could be played regularly. She asked if we could sell it anyway, even if it wouldn't bring much. I told her that the last one we offered brought only fifty dollars, but the man who bought it refused to pay for it. Finally, she said she had to get rid of it and that surely there was some use for it.

It was a common problem: what to say to clients when something they owned was worth very little or nothing, in this case a large fine-grained piano, quite valuable a hundred years earlier. I was tempted to say in jest that it would make a good anchor for a medium-sized fishing vessel but instead suggested she sell it with the house, which was on the market. I encouraged her to emphasize the beauty and rarity of the polished rosewood. She nodded in agreement.

Then she mentioned that most of the furnishings from the house were in storage in a downtown warehouse owned by the family. This sounded promising, but I hoped it would be something other than ragged Victorian sofas, partial sets of Limoges china displayed in a massive Empire sideboard, and similar leftovers for which there was usually little interest. Fulton, Robert, and I followed her in our truck to an old three-story brick building, "Mail Pouch Tobacco" still readable in faded paint two stories high on one side. Mrs. Sawyer invited us to take anything we wanted as this building also had to be emptied.

The furniture and accessories were stored in a large, dusty room on the ground floor. We found several pieces with acceptable auction potential: an oak rolltop desk, oak stack bookcases, a painted leather screen, and several humble paintings. Then, in the middle of a long, tight row of furniture, we found a small inlaid walnut chest. It had ogee bracket feet and vine-and-leaf inlay winding up both sides of the front beside the drawers. It was of small proportions—diminutive, we would say—almost always an asset. On the inventory, we wrote "small walnut chest," one of about fifteen items we listed.

I said that we would need to have the signatures of the other two heirs on the consignment agreement. Our client provided us with the necessary information, and we spoke with both heirs a few days later by phone to explain the consignment process and mention that their pieces would be sold a few weeks later in our July auction. They both seemed comfortable with the plans, and one of them, an elderly brother, said he hoped things would go "really well." They all signed the consignment agreement.

The chest was a late eighteenth- or early nineteenth-century American example. Furniture made prior to the Industrial Revolution and the onset of more mechanized furniture production was highly sought after, generally more so than later classical and Victorian styles. When we got home, we took out all the drawers, turned the chest upside down, and examined it with a strong light. It was in exceptional condition; the feet and glue blocks had not been altered, the delicate inlay was not a later addition, even the drawer runners had not been flipped, all features that increased its value. Its only flaw was that the original finish had been removed at some point, the surface now slightly oily and a bit dusty.

The chest did not immediately bring to mind any familiar New England forms. It did resemble several Pennsylvania examples, but not convincingly. We were tempted to attribute it to a Tennessee or Kentucky origin but knew of no examples to support such a claim; if it was Southern, it would be even more desirable. We wanted to do more research on the little chest and decided to hold it out of the July auction and offer it in our October sale. The other pieces consigned from the estate did well in the July sale, and the proceeds were divided among the three heirs, their checks mailed with a listing of the price realized for each item. Beside the "small walnut chest" was printed "October auction."

In the ensuing weeks, we showed the chest to many people; no one could make a clear attribution as to the region of origin, but all agreed it was a fine little piece. We went through the files at the Museum of Early Southern Decorative Arts in Winston-Salem but found no similar examples.

We pictured the chest in our auction brochure, and when people asked, we said our pre-sale estimate was $5,000–$10,000. When the chest came up in the auction, there were many bidders up to $15,000. After that, only two bidders were still active, one on the phone and one nervous woman in the gallery. The bidding climbed in $2,000 increments, the woman in the gallery bidding enthusiastically at first but then more slowly as it passed $30,000 and $40,000. The bidder on the phone was solid, never hesitating. At $50,000, the woman faltered, shook her head, and pulled her card down. I was about to say "sold" when she threw her card up and shouted, "$55,000." It was clearly her last fling at the little chest, but it failed. The phone bidder won the chest for $60,000.

The winning bidder was a scholar and collector from Kentucky who may have known the chest was of Kentucky origin. The underbidder, the woman in the gallery, said to me at a later auction, "I should have bought that cute little chest you had once. I think it was very rare." She was from Tennessee and may have believed it had been made in Tennessee.

About a week after the auction, one of the three heirs of the estate called, the gentleman who had hoped it would do "really well." He wondered what had happened to the "small walnut chest" listed on the consignment agreement. His voice carried a slight edge: "We never got paid for it." I explained that it had been moved to a later auction, it had just sold the week before, and his check would be issued in several days. I was pleased to let him know that it had done very well. I occasionally had unhappy news to report to an owner after an auction, so it was always a pleasure to deliver good news.

"What's 'very well'?"

"It brought $60,000."

After a long silence, he said, "Mr. Brunk, I'm elderly and don't hear very well. Could you say that again?"

"$60,000."

"Mr. Brunk, I have been told you are an honest man, and I don't mean to say you're not telling the truth, but could you say that again?"

"$60,000."

"Mr. Brunk, I don't have much income, and this is important to me. Could you please repeat that again, one number at a time?"

"Six, zero, zero, zero, zero."

"Mr. Brunk, OK, please do that one more time, and this time, please say when you get to the decimal point. I want to be sure I have it at the right place."

PIANO

Early in 1997, we were asked if we would be interested in selling a group of pianos that once belonged to televangelism's famous couple Jim and Tammy Faye Bakker. The pianos were stored at Heritage USA near Rock Hill, South Carolina, just south of Charlotte, North Carolina. Yes, we were interested, and several days later we left Asheville with a truck, a car, and a crew of six to evaluate the instruments.

During the three-hour drive from Asheville, my staff and I traded stories about what we knew or thought we knew of the Bakkers' very public life: their four condos in California, the gold plumbing fixtures, their matching Rolls-Royces. Robert said he'd heard that they'd owned an air-conditioned doghouse. We all laughed about Tammy Faye Bakker's reputation for excessive makeup and the once-popular white T-shirts sporting an explosion of black above the caption "I Ran into Tammy Faye at the Mall." We imagined what we would do if we suddenly held the Bakkers' immense wealth in our hands.

We were glad we had written directions, as there were no markings for Heritage USA along the road, even though in its heyday Heritage USA had been a small city, almost as large as Disney World, and included an amusement park, residences, a campground, TV studios, a golf course, a water park, and miles of roads. As we approached the 2,300-acre property, we saw in the distance the twenty-story hotel tower, a large rectangular stump rising from the otherwise featureless horizon. Over 165,000 donors had each given $1,000 toward its construction in return for future free lodging.

The entrance to the property was its own highway, two double lanes separated by a grass median. We stayed on the main highway, heading for the hotel tower.

The parking lot across from the entrance had turned into a field of crumbled asphalt; we stared and pointed like curious children as we passed a towering castle with an arcaded first floor. Then a cracked and faded sign appeared announcing the entrance to the golf course and what was once said to be the home of the world's largest Wendy's fast-food restaurant. The roads were lined with leaning, rusted iron fences, graffiti-decorated walls, and buildings with partially collapsed roofs, small trees growing from their gutters. The remnants of the water park, concrete animals and curving blue-and white-painted walls, stood dry.

At its peak in the mid-1980s, over 6 million people visited Heritage USA every year, but it was hard to imagine the noise and congestion of so many visitors to this weedy and rusty place. The decline began in 1987 when the personal life of Jim Bakker and the finances of his empire began to unravel. As if to add heavenly judgment to human frailty, the remnants of Hurricane Hugo passed through the area in the fall of 1989, causing great damage. The complex closed soon afterward, eight years before we arrived.

As we approached the hotel tower, we saw it was unfinished; large areas of brick facing had fallen off, one exposed place roughly the shape of Arkansas. Our guide met us at the white-columned entrance to a spacious reception area, part of a vast complex of shops, studios, offices, and lodging. A tall, friendly man received us warmly and mentioned that visitors were once greeted here by large chandeliers and gilt metal sconces hung in niches high above the floor. The walls were now lined with boxes and dusty office furniture.

After we shook hands, our guide led us to the studio where PTL (Praise the Lord) programs were produced. Beside the stage rested an unnamed, ten-foot white grand piano with extensive gilt carving, the first of seven grand pianos scattered throughout several buildings: a small chapel, other larger reception areas, and several storage buildings. We found a Kawai, two Baldwins, a Steinweg (an early Steinway), and two nineteenth-century pianos of unknown origin. As we located each piano, my crew evaluated how difficult each would be to load: how many dollies and piano boards would be needed, how many steps were involved, the necessary height of the loading dock.

We had been told that one of the grand pianos was a Bösendorfer, and I was eager to confirm that it was available for auction. Bösendorfer pianos have been made in Austria since the early nineteenth century and are renowned for their rich, colorful tones and for the nine extra keys at the lower end of the scale, originally added to the standard eighty-eight keys so that J. S. Bach organ transcriptions could be played. If the Bakkers were collecting pianos, this was surely the crown jewel. I had only heard of these magnificent instruments and never imagined we would one day sell one.

We found the Bösendorfer in a dim storage room with stacks of chairs and other bulky furniture. We slid the fitted cloth cover off the great piano and opened the hinged top, securing it with the wooden prop. From my earlier career as a woodworker, I recognized the fine book-matched, streaked black-and-deep-purple rosewood veneers, often a sign of skillful cabinetry. I pulled the piano bench into position and slowly lowered myself onto the tufted black leather seat. Though I'm not a pianist, I wanted to hear the hammers strike the strings and the sounding board magnify the waves of sound. My crew watched quietly. This instrument with its large turned legs, carved rosewood scrolls, and huge brass casters had the presence of a grounded, living thing, and I wanted to hear it speak. I played a few simple major chords, random minor chords, and simple scales. My hands wandered.

. . . .

In 1964, I attended Princeton Theological Seminary for a year. Then I moved to Hagerstown, Maryland, where I sang in the choir of an Episcopalian church. One Sunday morning, I sang a short solo in a longer work by Marc-Antoine Charpentier, about twenty notes spread over two words, *Christe eleison.* I practiced often as I was not used to singing solos. Those twenty majestic notes have stayed with me all my life. They always show up without notice; I find myself singing them to myself or, if alone, breaking into that superb entrance.

Those notes appeared when I sat down at the Bösendorfer. I hadn't planned to play them, but after the first quiet notes, my fingers quickly found them. The sounds were rich and layered: I could only imagine what music this piano might create in the hands of a skilled pianist. I told the man we would be happy to offer this fine instrument in an upcoming auction.

Several weeks later, on a cloudy day in early December, after completing the necessary contract, our crew loaded Jim and Tammy Faye Bakker's great

Bösendorfer piano onto our rental truck. We first removed the legs, then wrapped and secured the instrument on a piano board, and then slowly rolled our precious 800-pound cargo across the loading dock and onto the truck, guiding its passage from its previous life to whatever new venue lay ahead.

Our guide, eager for us to take everything left in the buildings, asked us to look around to see if there were other things we could offer at auction. He led us down a broad indoor pedestrian boulevard past storefronts and amusements, but all that remained were shells of the structures, recreations of nineteenth-century shops with reproduction cast-iron benches and dark-green streetlights—much like an abandoned movie set. It was a vast illusion: we were on Main Street, Heritage USA. We were witness to the remnants of expansive personal dreams in their worst possible moment, naked, stripped of all pretense, rationale, and use.

The Mennonite boy in me struggled with these expressions of wealth. That little boy might have asked what an amusement park, skating rink, golf course, and the world's largest Wendy's had to do with *church*. I kept thinking of those plain white Mennonite farmhouses, the homes of many of my twenty-five aunts and uncles, scattered through Ohio, Indiana, and Illinois, and the dining rooms of my childhood, with sturdy oak furniture, ironed and mended napkins and tablecloths, and muted homage paid to an inherited pressed glass bowl, badly chipped.

On the way to a large storage building, we were led through a smaller brick building and a large open room, perhaps converted warehouse space. Scattered stains marked the patched concrete floor, and several round industrial lights with wire grills hung from the high ceiling. The walls were lined with desks separated by plywood dividers, and each desk held an adding machine. Yellow foam cushions showed through the frayed upholstery of several office chairs. An empty canvas mail buggy rested beside each cubicle.

We were in the money room.

At their peak in the 1980s, Jim and Tammy Faye Bakker were seen in over 10 million homes. Tens of thousands of letters were opened here; as much as $1 million a week arrived in the mail. My staff, mostly strong, savvy young men used to loading heavy furniture, talked quietly and nodded as they gradually understood that great quantities of wealth had flowed through this place. Perhaps they wondered how it would feel to hold a stack of $100 bills in their hands. I imagined the staccato tabulations of the adding machines, the stacks of checks and cash growing on each shabby desk, earnest men and rubber-thumbed women flipping through the piles, counting, mail buggies filled and refilled. It was not intended that this room be seen by anyone except those who worked in it, and now quiet, it carried an air of sadness. Our voices and steps echoed slightly off the concrete floor. I wondered where the men and women were now and how they remembered their work, those who had counted those millions of dollars.

We walked into the adjacent storage building, crowded with pallets stacked four and five high: hundreds of boxes and crates, sagging from weight and time, brochures, calendars, books, small objects wrapped in plastic, photographs, promotional materials, maps, devotional guides perhaps free with a donation of any size—failed entrepreneurial Christianity. There were also thickets of artificial shrubs, rows of gold-painted urns, portable steps covered in purple velvet, easels, spotlights, iron arches, gold-framed mirrors, golf carts with flat tires, and whole municipalities of plastic flowers. In a corner, like a sulking child, sat a forklift, a pool of oil between its tires, as though it had relieved itself.

Like some of the pianos, much of what we saw was ornament, decoration to support the pretense of elegance and authenticity. Everything was covered with a thin, hazy layer, the fine silt of abandonment. Only the pianos were suitable for our auctions of fine and decorative arts. We would send another crew back with a larger truck for the remaining six instruments.

We were not responsible for removing the contents of the building, but what I saw was unnerving. Lodged in the Mennonite church's denial of the secular world was an inherent rejection of showy collections, mindless purchases, waste. I still carried elements of this critique of our culture. We were encouraged to be good stewards of all we had been given, materially and spiritually.

As I stood there surveying the room, I wondered if some of these things might be repaired or salvaged. Perhaps a load or two could be donated to Goodwill, but what of the rest? What would happen to this mountain of stuff? The many props to sustain this elaborate fiction were now only so much clutter. I imagined a row of idling dump trucks waiting for an oversize front-end loader to slide three mammoth bucketfuls into each empty truck. What would all this turn into, I wondered, as it lost form in a landfill, as it mixed with disposable diapers, unfixable outdoor grills, broken toys, and torn plastic shower curtains? How long would it be until the calendars and letterheads were not readable?

The crew and I returned to Asheville and over the next several weeks prepared for the next auction, displaying six of the seven grand pianos as parts of rooms—venues suggesting that this piano went well with this chest and that painting. Some displays were organized by period, such as late eighteenth-century British, or by color, such as an olive-green carpet with a painting and china of the same palette. In our galleries, with track lighting playing on fine paintings and furniture, our clients were encouraged to own these things, blurring the distinction between need and want.

But the seventh piano, the Bösendorfer, was displayed behind the eight-foot glass wall at the front of the Haywood Park Trade Mart, part of a downtown indoor arcade where we housed our business at the time. We trained several spotlights on its fine, rich surfaces. It was resplendent.

One day, as I walked by the piano, a woman tapped on the door, indicating she wished to speak with someone. She looked to be in her forties and wore sandals and pale blue socks. I opened the door and asked if I could be of any help.

She spoke quietly and said she had come by several times but not when anyone was around. "I'm sure you know how rare your Bösendorfer piano is," she added. Her eyes bounced in its direction. She added that she was a professional pianist and wondered if there was any chance she could play the piano for a few minutes. Her request was clear and unapologetic.

I told her the piano was slightly out of tune but that she was welcome to play it. I explained that people are always invited to play instruments during our previews, and we could call this an early preview.

She said she didn't need to own the Bösendorfer and would not be bidding on it when it came up at auction. "I hope that is OK. It would mean a great deal to me if I could just play it for a short while," she said again.

I reassured her that this was fine, as I invited her in and closed the door behind her. We walked toward the piano together. As she slowly circled it, her hand trailed on the rosewood surface. She sat down slowly, adjusting the height of the seat. Once she was comfortable, I excused myself to give her more privacy.

Four of us were working that day in an adjacent room, examining a collection of silver, writing catalog copy, and planning trips for the following week. First, she played part of a familiar Chopin nocturne. Then, a few quick portions of a Bach piece. I walked to the doorway and glanced at her. She played a few other fragments I didn't recognize, paused a bit, exhaled a long sigh, and then began her concert. In my memory, it was a piece by Brahms.

Slowly, like mounting waves, the sound cascaded and rolled through the room. It was the ocean. It was the wind groaning against rock cliffs. It was the whoosh of wings as 500 birds flew by. It was a conversation, then an argument between two lovers. We all gradually stopped working, only able to listen, our work no longer urgent.

There was a long silence when she finished about ten minutes later. Then Robert began clapping softly. He had no particular interest in classical music his tastes tended more toward the latest rock music but he recognized the skill and devotion of our guest, as did we all. I went out to open the door for her. She was walking slowly toward me, weeping, and waved her hand slightly in thanks.

When the Bösendorfer came up for auction several weeks later, it was purchased by a local physician who wanted a first-rate piano for his home. He prevailed over several phone bidders in the United States and Europe and paid over $42,000, a fair price at the time. The great rosewood piano still rests quietly in the music room of his spacious home, where, I am told, he occasionally plays a few old jazz tunes for himself.

....

One summer, eight years after the sale of the Bösendorfer piano, I flew to the Sierra Nevada mountains in California to participate in a vision quest, a Native American experience designed to create signs that might suggest guidance in one's life. The first day, with thirty pounds on my back, I hiked with twelve other people to a remote camping site beside a small glacial lake, at an altitude of about 10,000 feet. After we unpacked our gear, we were instructed to introduce ourselves to the mountains, the earth, the lake, and the sky. I walked around for an hour, trying to enter a world very different from the one I had left. I ended up standing on a large flat stone beside the lake. As I looked at the mountains, lake, and sky, I realized I was crying—quiet, painless tears. From out of my mouth came the "Christe eleison" I had sung in the church in Maryland and played on the Bösendorfer piano. I was startled by my voice, strong and clear as it bounced off the nearby stone peaks.

This is what music does. It enables us to place markers in the landscapes of our memory—some bright flags waving in a slight breeze, others weathered sticks we one day push into the ground in hopes that this little string of notes will always be there for us to enjoy again, in moments of grace and joy. I hum those twenty notes as I write these words.

The Bösendorfer piano, a monument of coherence and purpose and an instrument capable of creating remarkable music, had rested beside a building filled with waste, the last remains of the Bakkers' crumbling empire. But this piano, perhaps above all else, had survived the collapse of their dreams. Perhaps the Bakkers could have found a measure of satisfaction if they knew that the original purpose of the Bösendorfer, to create beautiful music, has been achieved many times and that it had even created a moment of reverence when Charpentier's "Christe eleison" was played.

I understand so little of this.

BEAD

The house looked like all the other small residences on the street, housing for textile workers from the 1950s. The owner, Mrs. Chandler, a woman in her seventies, wearing a colorful apron and fluffy slippers, welcomed us into her small five-room bungalow. She walked with some difficulty, favoring her right leg or foot. She said she was in the midst of a difficult transition: her declining health and growing medical expenses were forcing her to sell her house and its contents; she needed money and had no other assets. She planned to move to Florida and live with her sister.

In 1999, Fulton and I had traveled to Elizabethton, Tennessee, where Mrs. Chandler and her parents had worked in the rayon mills. She said her ancestors had lived in East Tennessee since the early nineteenth century and she hated to leave the area but had no choice. She believed her house was worth about $30,000 and hoped to raise a similar amount with the sale of her antiques. This was not a case of downsizing and selling less desirable pieces; she was counting on this sale to pay off debts and cover moving expenses.

Her home was clean and orderly, filled with the rewards of careful collecting: graniteware, carnival glass, flow-blue china, baskets, oak furniture. As we slowly walked through her rooms, she often picked up a piece and told us where she had found it and why she had bought it. I quickly realized that the value of her antiques would probably fall far short of her expectations. She had no outstanding oak furniture, mostly plain tables and plant stands; no ornate, bow-front china cabinets or side-lock chests. She had none of the rare colors or patterns of carnival glass, much of the flow-blue had small chips or cracks, and the graniteware collection was mostly modern reproductions. The care with which she had decorated her home would not translate into much money; she had bought what she could afford, often pieces with flaws.

After our tour of her house, we sat in her living room to discuss her situation. I wanted to gently lower her expectations about the value of her collections and told her that the market for some of her pieces was weak; a chip or a crack could make a big difference.

As I glanced around the room, I saw something in a dim frame hanging near the oil heater. Mrs. Chandler said it was an old Indian bag that had come down in her family, and she explained that one of her ancestors had been a soldier in the US Army in the 1840s. He was stationed in Virginia and witnessed the decimation of the Indian population; many were starving or had died of yellow fever. Her ancestor had befriended a group of Indians, and he had bought a cow and delivered it to them so they would have food to eat. He was given the beaded bag as a gift from the grateful Indians. This gift and the story had been passed down through four generations to Mrs. Chandler.

She said we could look at the bag if we wished. Fulton then lifted the bag and its frame off the wall so we could examine it. The shoulder bag, sometimes called a bandolier bag, was made of cloth and fully decorated with glass beads in patterns of vines, delicate flowers, tassels, and eagles. It was an exquisite, old example of Indian beadwork, in good condition and unquestionably of high value. I said we would be pleased to offer it in an upcoming auction. She replied that she had never considered selling it; she thought of it as a "family piece" rather than something worth a lot of money, but she was willing to sell it if it "brought a good price." She agreed to let us take the bag to evaluate and estimate its value if we offered it at auction. I assured her that I would be in touch with her for her approval before we sold it.

Then, almost as an afterthought, she mentioned that she had a tape recording of her mother recounting the story of the soldier and the cow. I quickly asked if it would be possible for her to play the tape for us. She slowly walked to the bedroom and returned with a small cassette player, carrying it cautiously with both hands. Mrs. Chandler and I sat beside each other on the sofa, Fulton on a nearby chair. Mrs. Chandler quickly found her mother's account, cleared her throat, and bowed her head slightly in a posture suggesting reverence, as if here, in this humble home in rural Tennessee, the contents of an ancient reliquary were about to be revealed.

The three of us stared at the cassette player on Mrs. Chandler's lap as her mother's confident but scratchy voice recounted the story of the beaded bag. The recording matched Mrs. Chandler's account almost to the word, as though it might have been memorized from frequent retelling. I noted that the word "decimated" appeared again, and most importantly, this version named the soldier, Landon Carter. She played the recording several times as I quickly took notes.

I was charged with excitement. Most stories about the origins of a rare object are difficult to confirm, but this information was promising, more specific and credible than many stories I had heard. Mrs. Chandler had also not embellished the story to inflate its potential value, as was often the case in these situations. We talked a while longer about her family's history, then Fulton and I thanked Mrs. Chandler for her hospitality and for playing the tape. We carefully packed the bag and its frame and headed back to Asheville.

Many pieces of Native American art that come to auction are skillful reproductions of older pieces, but scholars and collectors in this field to whom I sent photos of the beaded bag were unanimous: this piece was authentic and rare. It was made in the early nineteenth century and, according to one collector, was probably Muscogee (Creek Nation) or Lenni Lenape (Delaware Nation). Three of the people I sent photos to expressed an interest in bidding on the bag if it came up for auction.

I called Mrs. Chandler about two weeks later to share what I had learned. I told her that my auction estimate, based on recent sales of similar examples of Indian beadwork, would be $10,000–$15,000, with the potential to sell for even more. She was pleased and said I should go ahead and put the bag in the next auction.

But I felt a growing uneasiness as discussions of selling the beaded bag were becoming a reality. I explained that this was an irreplaceable historic artifact in her family, and I wanted her to be very sure she wanted to sell it, even if it was worth a lot of money. I said I would be pleased to offer it for her, but an auction is a one-way street, I warned; she and her family would never have it back. I realized that a part of me wanted Mrs. Chandler to keep together this rare family inheritance and the story of its history.

Continuing our phone conversation, I explained that the beaded bag was a microcosm of personal and regional history, and it connected her to her family's history in Carter County, Tennessee, to Landon Carter, and to the homelands of Native Americans in the area. Without the bag, the story could drift into insignificance. Many times, all we have are the stories, but this time we had both, the story and the object.

Mrs. Chandler said she had thought about this often since I had visited her, and she acknowledged that the beaded bag was indeed a family treasure. "But I don't really have any choice," she said evenly. She wanted to move to Florida to be with her sister and had no other way to get there. She said I should go ahead and sell the beaded bag. I acceded to her wishes and promised her we would do our best when we offered it at auction.

Man's beaded cloth hand-sewn shoulder bag, possibly Creek or Delaware, strap 54½ × 7¼ in., bag 9½ (opens to 16½ in.) × 10½ in., strap with stylized red and blue flowers on light blue field, other half with stylized leaves with dark red over light blue with meandering vine and yellow blossoms throughout, all with white borders, each end with three tapered tassels approximately 6½ in., bag with stylized eagles, dark red beads with diamond shaped blue centers on dark purple and light blue/purple field, dark blue back cloth probably wool, back of strap with printed red diamond design, liner of bag with similar diamond-fleck design, hem probably silk hem tape with considerable wear and losses, scattered bead loss particularly on tassels, considerable loss to single row of white eagle beads, pouch has stylized V-shaped flap with two eagles on front of bag and one eagle on flap.

The beaded bag sold for $50,600. When I called Mrs. Chandler that night to tell her the good news, she was overjoyed and said she couldn't believe how well it had done, more than her house and its contents might have been worth. She was still planning to move to Florida, but this took all the pressure off her situation. "It makes my life possible," she said with gratitude.

I suggested she make copies of the tape recording and give them to regional museums, historical societies, and any local archives as a way to keep the story of the bag alive and available. I said I would also send her photos of the bag so she would have a visual record of it.

I was attracted to the symmetry of the story. Sometime in the nineteenth century, a soldier gave a cow to a group of Native Americans in need of food and, undoubtedly, saved several lives. In gratitude, they gave the soldier a gift, a beaded bag. About 150 years later, a fourth-generation descendant of the soldier, a woman in need, sold the bag for enough money to "make my life possible."

But, I reflected, this was still just a story. I wondered how much of this had really happened. As with many oral histories, the story may have been based on fragments of an actual event and, over many years, been added to and subtracted from by imaginative storytellers, the narrative now a collage of popular folklore and easy stereotypes: destitute people, generous soldier, skillful beadwork, gifts exchanged, gratitude.

I wondered if there was any way to confirm the story with historical records: a soldier named Landon Carter, in Virginia in the 1840s, possibly with connections to Native Americans. Could we find written proof of this remarkable oral history?

The historical record for Virginia and eastern Tennessee mentions many Landon Carters. Colonel Landon Carter I (1710–78), a prominent planter in Richmond County, Virginia, had a son who bore his name, Landon Carter II (1738–1801), and a grandson, Landon Carter III (1757–1820). In northeastern Tennessee, Carter County was named after a General or Captain Landon Carter (1760–1800) who fought in the Revolutionary War. Elizabethton, the county seat, was named after his wife, Elizabeth. We had been sitting in a home in Elizabethton when Fulton lifted the bag off the wall.

As I wrote this account several years later, I turned to my brother, Stan, who has done extensive research on the history of our family and whose skills in this sort of investigation far exceeded mine. He found a Landon Carter who, during the Civil War, had served in the Confederate army in Virginia and a second Landon Carter who had served in the Union army in Tennessee.

Stan decided to look for what he called the "beaded bag Landon Carter" by beginning with the woman who had consigned the bag and working back, looking for an ancestor named Landon Carter. The consignor's husband's first name was Landon, so Stan began with his ancestors. Four generations earlier, across several family lines, he came to Landon C. Carter, 1826–96, the one who had served in the Union army and who, during the Civil War, had worked hard to root the Confederates out of the state of Tennessee. But Stan could not find any evidence that this Landon Carter lived or worked in Virginia or had any contact with Indians. He could find no other verification of the story.

Yet the story is its own truth, a living narrative that may not require proof in the written record. For about 150 years, the story has been a valued oral history, a repeated chronicle that helped these families understand their histories and the traditions that had created the texture of their lives. It validated the agonies of Native American displacement, and one carefully preserved fragment, the beaded bag, became a fulcrum in their understanding of those events. The story asks that this sequence, these gifts, be remembered. I have become the next contributor to the conservation of this account, and as I pass this unique glimpse of Tennessee history on to you, you also become part of the story.

The existence of the beaded bag prompted many other questions. In what social context was the bag created? Had it been a gift between several people or tribes before it was given to Landon Carter? Did the beadwork, flowers, eagles, color choices, and designs reflect any specific symbols or traditions? Who wove the cloth? Who, in the telling of the story, had first used the word "decimated"?

I had contact information for the party that purchased the beaded bag in the 1999 auction, and I wondered if they had done any research or had any additional information about the bag. But despite many inquiries, I was unable to contact them.

For me, the beaded bag carried the shadows of the hundreds of thousands of Native Americans who lost their land to European settlers, lost the structure and the sustainability of their cultures, and lost their means of survival. I thought about President Andrew Jackson's Indian Removal Act of 1830, causing the displacement of 40,000 Native Americans in five Nations in the southeastern United States to "Indian Territory" in Oklahoma. In an address to Congress on December 6, 1830, Jackson referred to the Indian population as "wandering savages" and stated that "the Central Government kindly offers him a new home, and proposes to pay the whole expense of his removal and settlement."

The Tsalagihi Ayeli (Cherokee) were forced to abandon their homes and 24 million acres of land.

....

In 2020, a friend and I often enjoyed exploring remote gravel roads in the mountains of far-Western North Carolina. On one such fall day, we found ourselves on a steep winding road, having begun slightly southwest of Robbinsville, then headed south over the ravines and ridges of the Snowbird Mountains to Andrews. On old maps, the road was known as the Old Army Road; on newer maps, Long Creek Road.

On this clear, brilliant day beside a mountain stream, the air carried the scent and rustle of swirling water. Colorful maple and birch leaves floated silently to the earth, a tranquil setting to satisfy one's needs for solitude and gratitude.

But partway up the mountain, a sign beside the road announced that this road had been part of the Trail of Tears. This is where Andrew Jackson's Indian Removal Act of 1830 played out, in this peaceful forest on the Old Army Road. We parked in a deep bed of fall leaves. This road was built in the 1830s to make it possible to drive the Cherokee from their ancestral homelands. They were rounded up like stray cattle and imprisoned in stockades built in Robbinsville, known then as Fort Montgomery, and in Andrews, known then as Fort Delaney, then to Murphy, the army's regional headquarters, Fort Butler.

The Removal Act applied to the Chikasha (Chickasaw), Chahta Achvffa (Choctaw), Myskoke (Muscogee-Creek), yat'siminoli (Seminole), and Cherokee Nations and authorized the federal government to extinguish any Indian title to any land claims in southeastern United States.

The many well-developed archaeology sites in the region document the presence of the Cherokee on this land for 400 years and aboriginal habitation in this region at least as early as the Archaic period, 4000–2000 BC.

The Cherokee were the last of the five Nations to be "removed" in the late 1830s.

It was estimated that 4,000 Cherokee lost their lives on the Trail of Tears, many to starvation, exposure, and exhaustion and from contact with communicable diseases. Hundreds, if not thousands, of Cherokee families began their 800-mile journey to Oklahoma here on this road, many on foot and in manacles. They left behind their houses, farms, gardens, and many of their animals.

As we sat among the trees that fall day, we tried to imagine the scene 170 years earlier: a ragged procession of horse-drawn stagecoaches and wagons, elderly people and children, many with walking sticks, everyone carrying something, and all moving in the same direction to an unknown land, the air now thick with confusion, fear, and sadness. Where did people rest? What did they eat? A galactic tragedy of unspeakable cruelty.

Many Cherokee were driven from their homes at gunpoint and had little time to prepare. What artifacts or family treasures made by their ancestors might they have been forced to leave behind? I hadn't thought of the beaded bag for several years, but suddenly it was there, hovering in my haunted imagination. How many Cherokee had been unable to keep a similar cherished object: a soapstone bowl, a decorated earthenware jar, a pottery effigy figure of an animal, a woven river cane mat? Looters often followed the federal troops and ransacked the homes and farms of the Cherokee.

ARCHIVE

On very warm day in August 2001, three other appraisers and I greeted a crowd of people who had filled a small gymnasium near Augusta, Georgia. The event was an appraisal day for a local nonprofit agency. Midafternoon, a friendly older woman with a handsome low-country accent came to my table. She wore white strap sandals and a bright summer dress accented by small gold pendant earrings. She smiled and said how kind it was of me to come to this event and look at people's antiques. "For many years," she began, "we have wanted to talk with someone about an old chest we have, someone who might know something about it." From a large black purse, the size of a small suitcase, she dug out a pack of photos. Publicity for this promotion had encouraged people to bring photos of large pieces, objects too awkward or heavy to move about.

She pointed toward her husband, who stood several steps away, his back against the table for support, saying that he, Ollie—short for Oliver—had taken most of the photographs. He waved in my direction, one hand making small arcs in the manner of a windshield wiper. He wore black loafers but no socks, his thin white legs showing several inches below the cuffs of his corduroy pants. He smiled slightly through his deeply creased face as he watched the stream of people and their possessions come and go.

"Before we look at the photos, we want to tell you about the chest," she directed. I was eager to see the photos, but as was often the case, the story came first.

She explained that this "Charleston chest" had been in her family for at least five generations and that in the early nineteenth century, her great-great-grandfather owned a rice plantation on the Ashley River. The chest was made of boards from a great walnut tree that stood in the side yard of the big house, and when the tree went over in a storm sometime in the early 1800s, her great-great-grandfather decided to make two chests from the lumber in that tree, one for each of his sons. One of the sons was her great-grandfather on that side of her family.

Her arms trembled slightly as she gestured with her hands held wide apart, saying that the tree was "that big around." Her husband, still at the far end of the table, nodded several times as she spoke. I wanted to ask several questions but didn't interrupt.

"You know," she declared, "those logs from that tree were so big and heavy, it took two big draft horses to drag them to the saw pit." She asked if I knew what a saw pit was, but before I could say yes, I was familiar with them, she continued, saying that back in those days, before steam engines and water-powered sawmills, boards were sawed from a log above a long pit, one man above and one below, sawing by hand with a long saw, and that her ancestors had dug a pit on their plantation and had their enslaved workers saw out the lumber. She added that the chest had been hers ever since she and Ollie got married.

With no preface, I wedged myself into the conversation. "Pit-sawed lumber is very easy to identify because of the distinctive marks left by the saw. I'm eager to see the backboards of your chest." I counseled myself to be patient.

She smiled and said we would get to the photos in a minute, but she wanted to say something else before we did. "Mr. Brunk, I imagine you have heard a lot of stories that people have made up about some old antique of theirs, but I want you to know that this is a true account of where our chest came from." She said her grandfather had heard the story all his life, and he had passed it on to her before he died. "We were standing in the dining room of my house, looking at the chest, when he told me all this."

With that, she pulled one photo from the stack and laid it on the table. "This is the bottom drawer of the chest. When I was a little girl, the chest sat in the dining room of the big house, and we kept our second-best silver in that bottom drawer." She closed her eyes occasionally as if to focus on the details and explained that she and her sister often sat on the floor and played house with the silver, pretending to be setting a table for elegant guests. They used demitasse spoons, pickle forks, and individual butter knives for the silverware, silver saucers for plates, finger bowls for entrées, and upside-down goblets for centerpieces or candlesticks. She paused, seeing again the tiny place settings scattered on the yellow pine floor. "We had such a grand time in those days." For the first time, she slowed down, drifting further into her shining memories.

Finally, she pulled the rubber band off the photos and spread them out on the table, like a deck of cards. Ollie picked up one, a front view of the chest, and said that during the Civil War, the plantation had been a makeshift hospital for Confederate soldiers and that supplies, such as they were, had been stored in the chest: medicine in the three small drawers across the top, bandages and surgical implements in the three large drawers below. "You know, those were difficult times for people, and everyone did what they could to make life a little easier." He now stood beside his wife and rested a hand lightly on her shoulder. He called her Millie as he spoke.

I suddenly realized that Millie and Ollie were tired of standing, so I invited them to pull out the two chairs on their side of the table and rest a bit. They both thanked me as they lowered themselves onto the chairs.

Ollie described how everyone in Millie's family had pitched in to help in the hospital: carrying and heating water, cooking, gathering food in the garden and orchards, washing clothes in the big iron pots beside the summer kitchen, and occasionally helping with burials in the small cemetery on a nearby hillside. He said Millie came from a hardworking family, and he always admired how she pitched in to help anyone in need.

I listened to more stories as they sifted through the photos: the time they had hidden money in a drawer to pay a debt; the way they had to chisel into the chest when they lost the key; the evening when her family entertained the governor of South Carolina and wine was spilled on the chest, red stains still visible; the mysterious writing on the bottom of a drawer, discovered by a child; and how the chest was covered with flowers when a double wedding was held in the parlor.

They had not encouraged me to look at the photos, but I had glanced at many of them while they spoke. Ollie's detailed photos were very helpful.

Their chest was not made in Charleston, nor was it made in this country; it was a British chest, the primary wood mahogany, not walnut. No labeled or documented Charleston chests from the Federal period, made of walnut, have ever been found. The drawer bottoms were perpendicular to the drawer fronts with a supporting brace down the middle, the interior had built-in dust panels, and the backboards were fitted, unlike most American examples. All these features suggested a British origin.

But how could I possibly present them with this information, daring to challenge all they had told me? I didn't know if I could find a way to do this and hesitated to say anything about my findings.

As they continued to relive their memories, I increasingly realized that their stories were what bound them to the place where they lived, and to each other, more essential to them than dust panels or bracket feet. In their retelling of their stories, they could revisit the people and events that had shaped the landscapes of their lives: the furrows, the springs, the stone boundary markers.

On this particular day, they needed an audience. My work, my responsibility, was to listen, to be a witness, to affirm the value of their stories by my presence. The specific details of their lives were more urgent to them than the chest, about which they never asked.

To fit the carefully arranged narrative by which they understood their personal histories in that place, the chest had to be made of boards from the walnut tree beside the big house. The chest had to have held bandages during the Civil War and had to have been made by enslaved people to conform to the exalted mythology of the region, as now owning a chest made by enslaved craftsmen was a source of pride for the few who possessed such a thing.

Millie cleared her throat and, without looking, sent out a hand to search for Ollie's arm. She struggled for composure. "We are moving into a retirement community in a few months, and our little apartment won't have room for the chest. None of our children or grandchildren have room for such a large, heavy piece of furniture."

She said their church had a program to help immigrant families find housing and get settled. "We have two Mexican women who help us with housekeeping, and we love them dearly. We are going to donate the chest to that program at our church. We need to have a short written description of the chest and a value for it when we donate it." She said they were hoping I could help them with that.

I glanced at the two of them. Suddenly, they seemed much older, almost frail, their movements more hesitant, their smiles requiring more effort. Had they aged as they told their stories, or did I see and hear them more clearly now that the chest had faded in importance?

The chest was an archive, an anthology of the many oral histories it activated. If the chest was gone from their lives, they would still have the stories, refreshed and possibly embellished with each retelling. As they told me their stories, they were rehearsing, preparing to live without the chest.

On a clean sheet of paper, I wrote, "A late 18th or early 19th century British, mahogany, line inlaid, six-drawer chest with dovetailed drawers, bracket feet, and brass drawer pulls, in good condition, $1,500. Robert S. Brunk, August 11, 2001." I placed the description in a manila folder, handed it to them, and suggested they store it in one of the drawers of the chest for safekeeping. Millie slid the folder into her purse, though neither she nor Ollie had looked at the document. I was prepared to discuss the chest if they had any questions. They looked at me with kindness in their eyes but said no, they had no questions. They thanked me profusely, nodding, smiling, relief in their voices.

I wondered if they knew their chest was not made on the family's plantation. If so, perhaps they wanted to protect the truth of their stories, the reassurance of familiar litanies they recounted to each other. There may have been no reason to rewrite the specific language of those litanies, the stories that would offer them comfort and sanctuary for the rest of their days. They gathered up their photos and slowly walked away.

APPRAISAL

In the fall of 2001, a South Carolina television station decided to host a free appraisal event. Bring in those curious objects in your attic and basement you have always wondered about; they may be very valuable, the announcements repeatedly suggested. The surging interest in *Antiques Roadshow*, in which unsuspecting people expressed real or feigned surprise at the great value of their old painting or odd piece of furniture, had many watchers curious about their unusual doorstop or strange carving of a dog. I was one of seven appraisers enlisted to evaluate the treasures people had brought in. I often wished the *Roadshow* spent more time showing pieces of little value.

A traffic jam near the convention center delayed my nine o'clock arrival on this Saturday morning. When I saw the TV station's helicopter shooting live coverage of a line of people a block long, I realized those folks were waiting for appraisals.

I found my place in an arc of tables near the center of the arena and organized my equipment: a soft cover for the table, portable light, magnifying glasses, black light, reference books, water, and several granola bars.

I noticed that one of the other appraisers had a small sign on her table with a hand-drawn smiling face: "The only person interested in what your grandmother had was your grandfather."

A long, distended procession quickly formed about ten feet in front of my table: people of all persuasions and means holding old dolls, beer steins, cut glass bowls; others had unopened boxes and bags. One man clutched an old clock. Some scraped floor lamps and unusual chairs along the concrete floor as the line slowly shuffled forward.

These events were always hard work. Very often, the pieces people brought in were not rare or something they could easily convert to significant cash. I would need to find pleasant ways to explain this to the participants, not easy going when they believed otherwise and had waited several hours to have their object evaluated. I braced myself and tried to visualize loving-kindness for all mankind.

I had no idea this was the opening moment of a twelve-hour marathon.

Figurine

A young man who looked to be in his thirties, wearing a frayed Clemson sweatshirt and unlaced boots, walked quickly to my table. He smiled weakly through his uneasy face.

With two hands he positioned a large metal figurine on my table, a slender, demure young lady, draped in a flowing gown furled by a slight breeze, both arms outstretched at her sides, her pose and low neckline mildly suggestive. "I want to know how much this bronze is worth. I know it's valuable," he announced. He rotated it so that the woman faced me. He said he had inherited the figurine several years earlier from a wealthy aunt who had insured it for "a lot of money" and kept it on a rare, antique marble stand. She had told him to take good care of this unusual gift, but he had decided to sell the "sexy lady." I introduced myself and thanked him for bringing it in.

I picked up the figurine, about eighteen inches tall, and could immediately tell that it was far too light to be a bronze. I explained that this was known as spelterware, an alloy of zinc and lead, often used to make inexpensive copies of well-known bronze figures in the late nineteenth and early twentieth centuries. I handed it to him and said that if it were bronze, it would be much heavier, more difficult to lift. He tested the weight a bit before setting it down, frowned, but said nothing.

Using a strong light, I inspected the piece and saw a signature on the base, just below the woman's gown. "Moreau," it read, visible in raised script. "It's Auguste Moreau," the young man said quickly. "I took it by an antique shop, and they looked it up for me. He was French, and his bronzes are valuable, but they wouldn't say what she was worth."

Looking for positive words, I said he was correct; Moreau was famous for his bronze sculptural figures.

I found two old solder scars on the back of the woman, probably where some arrangement of lights had been attached. I explained that many of these pieces from the Art Nouveau period were made as lamps, when electric lamps were still something of a novelty, and this might have had two or more lights fastened where the scars were visible. This damage lowered the value of the figurine, but, I noted, in its day this lamp would have been very impressive, the fancy lady holding ornate lights.

"I know it used to be a lamp," he protested, "but there is no damage to the lady."

I asked if he was interested in the retail value of the figurine. He gathered himself a bit, as if to gain authority. "Before you make your offer," he began, "I know your game. You've been trying to find fault with it so you won't offer me much, but I know she's worth a lot, and I'm not going to give her away."

"I'm not planning on making an offer," I replied, "and I don't have any desire to take advantage of you." I explained that this was an appraisal event and that it would be unethical for an appraiser to make offers. I added that we had also been instructed not to buy anything from the participants.

"So, you aren't going to buy her?" he asked, his expectations fading as he pushed his hands into his jeans' pockets.

"No, I'm not going to buy it," I said quietly. He slowly picked up the figurine, stared at it for a moment, and then quickly walked away across the congested concrete floor. People watched him, perhaps not encouraged by his obvious despair, wondering if they, too, would be disappointed when it was finally their turn.

An hour later, I saw him moving toward me, past the noisy line. He came to my table and stood to one side, waiting for the person talking with me to finish. As she left, he jumped in front of the table, ignoring the next gentleman in line. Several people glared at him as he shoved the figurine onto the table.

He leaned in, close, his face now slack, his breath faintly rancid. "I couldn't find anyone who would buy it," he said in a whisper just short of pleading. "I'm down on my luck. Could you just help me out and give me five dollars for her?"

I was tempted by his specific, unpretentious plea, but as I shook my head, I could not think of any way to help him. He turned away quickly, clearly embarrassed to have asked. I watched him walk toward the nearest exit, his steps uneven, his body slightly bent, as though he faced a ceaseless headwind. He gripped the spelterware lady by the waist with one hand and held her at his side, parallel to the floor.

A few minutes later, after he was out of sight, I thought of what I might have done: I could have wadded up a five-dollar bill and dropped it on the floor when he was not watching and then pointed to it, saying that he had dropped something. It might have eased his dilemma a bit and avoided any further indignity.

Rug

The next man in line, a friendly older man wearing a faded denim jacket, rolled out a Navajo rug on my table. He held a Christie's catalog for an auction of Native American material and said he had found it in a pile of free books in a public library. He opened to a specific page and pointed to a photograph. "My rug looks a lot like this one," he said, smiling. "And since it brought $55,000, I'm hoping mine might be worth a lot too." He said he had always been interested in Navajo rugs.

I almost always enjoy a detailed examination of a promising object, and he seemed genuinely curious about his rug, so after I introduced myself, we spent some time comparing his rug to the Christie's example.

The differences were significant. The Christie's rug was a second-phase chief's blanket from the 1880s, the man's rug a loosely woven twentieth-century version, made fifty or sixty years later. I explained that because of the decimation of Indian sheep herds in the nineteenth century, Navajo weavers used what materials they could find, including yarn from other textiles, which were loosened and rewoven with other fabrics. The Christie's example had several areas of this "raveled yarn," very desirable to collectors. Most of the Christie's rug was also woven with vegetal dyes rather than later synthetic dyes, and small areas showed the use of cochineal dye made from dried red beetles, also scarce and highly sought-after.

We examined his rug carefully and found no evidence of raveled yarn or any of the rare dyes. Instead, we found small areas of scattered moth damage, pet urine stains, and a few clumsy repairs. The design of his rug, however, was a faithful and accurate depiction of a chief's blanket. I complimented him for identifying his rug among the many similar examples in the Christie's catalog. We looked through it and discussed other unusual examples, most in the $5,000–$10,000 range.

"Well," he commented, "I guess my rug isn't worth very much." His voice reflected mild disappointment but not surprise.

I replied that if his rug were in excellent condition, it would be in the $300–$500 range and in its current condition would still be worth between $50 and $100. He smiled the smile of someone who had just found a real bargain. "Well, I came out all right. I paid a dollar for it at a flea market." I thanked him for bringing it in and encouraged him to keep looking for good Navajo textiles.

Print

Several hours later, the line no shorter, a well-dressed woman, probably in her sixties, approached my table; the silver bracelets on one arm extended halfway to her elbow. She hoisted a framed work of art onto the table and stated with imposing certainty, "I looked up this artist, and her paintings are worth $10,000 to $20,000." She mentioned that an appraiser had also looked at it several years ago and told her it was "valuable."

I saw bright, multicolored flowers arranged in a round yellow vase, but I also saw that this was not a painting but an offset print, a reproduction of a still life by Jane Peterson, a well-known twentieth-century American artist. The composition frame, molded to imitate a carved wooden frame, had been finished with a dark stain and had little value.

The owner of the print watched impatiently as I quickly looked up auction records for Jane Peterson's still life paintings of similar size featuring flowers, and yes, I explained to her, if it were a painting, it could be worth several thousand dollars. She glared at me, her hands on her hips.

"It's not a painting?"

I explained that this still life had been printed on paper by a four-color process; there was no paint and no canvas. She bristled. "This has hung in my living room for many years and has been admired by many people. We have always called it a painting." She said she sometimes sat in a chair and just stared at the colorful zinnias, her favorite flowers.

"You are very observant," I remarked, saying that Jane Peterson was well-known for her paintings of flowers and included zinnias in many of her works.

We had recently sold a limited-edition Jane Peterson print, and I had become familiar with her work. I noted that Peterson had even written a book about how to paint flowers. I mentioned that some of her most valuable works pictured harbor scenes in Gloucester, Massachusetts, and that she had also had work exhibited in Europe. On a personal note, I pointed out that Peterson grew up in Elgin, Illinois, near where I grew up. But none of my efforts to shift the conversation were successful; she would have none of it.

"I still think it's a painting," she declared, annoyed and out of breath.

I laid the print flat on the table and examined the surface with a magnifying glass; the dots of an offset print were immediately clear. I explained how the print had been made and encouraged her to look at it with the magnifying glass. She fumbled with the unfamiliar device for a moment but said nothing. I asked if she saw any brushstrokes or paint.

"All right, if it is a print, what is it worth?" Her voice was insistent, brittle.

I knew this print with its fake wood frame could be bought new in a discount store for under ten dollars or at a yard sale for even less. "I think you should just enjoy it and not worry about the dollars and cents." I suggested that she could still enjoy the bright flowers pictured in the print.

Infuriated, almost shouting, she demanded, "I want the number. What is it worth?" Her voice carried a note of fear, a slight current of dread under the waves of her anger.

I paused, searching for something redemptive to say, but finding nothing, I said quietly, "The number is two dollars."

She gripped the print by one side of the frame and ran from the place, the zinnias waving in great arcs, in cadence with her aggravated stride. Several people waiting in line backed up a bit as she stormed by.

Perhaps I should not have challenged her belief that she owned a fine painting. I could have lied about it being a print and made up a number, say $10,000, so she could then own her beliefs. Whatever joy or dreams she imagined for herself would have been available to her. Could she have breathed more easily?

Would this information have changed her life in other ways? Perhaps people would then understand that she had a discerning eye, that she owned valuable objects. Maybe she would experience more clarity and direction in her life; her relationships would now be more rewarding. Would she have found quiet times to be thankful for her life?

Arrowhead

Around one o'clock, the appraisers were given a short break while volunteers stood behind our tables. My volunteer arrived, carrying a plate of food. I put the food down on my table and made a quick dash toward a restroom.

A young man wearing an oversize tank top saw me and galloped across the floor on a diagonal course to intersect me just as I reached for the door of the men's room. I told him I would be out in a minute.

"You're one of the appraisers, aren't you?" he half shouted when I exited. Two or three people in the crowded entrance to the restroom had apparently heard the word "appraiser" and quickly jumped behind him, each holding something to be appraised, forming a short new line. He thrust out a rough hand that held several small quartzite arrowheads. "I don't mean to bother you, but what are these arrowheads worth?"

I looked at them briefly. "Where did you find them?"

"In a plowed field after it rained."

"They were in disturbed ground, which lowers their value. They might be worth a dollar or two each. Most of them have broken tips."

"I see them at the flea market for a lot more than that. There's a man who always has a lot of arrowheads on his table."

"If they were mine, I would take them to the man you saw at the flea market and see what he would give you for them."

I hurried back to my table.

Pewter

By 8:00 p.m., the line had thinned and no longer spilled out of the building. Many people, weary from standing, had found odd chairs, boxes, crates, and other improvised seats they pushed along as the line slowly crept forward. A few were reading newspapers or magazines, but others had left, undoubtedly exhausted by the long wait. Kind gestures and patience were in short supply.

A woman, standing at the table of another appraiser, suddenly shrieked in joy, crying, waving her hands in excited gestures, like a player at a row of slot machines watching money spill out onto the floor. Apparently, she had hit the jackpot with the piece of silver she had brought in. Others in line watched at a distance, only a few of them smiling at her apparent good fortune. How nice, I thought, that someone heard good news today.

At eleven, only four appraisers were still examining the curious array of possessions people had brought in. Three appraisers had departed, presumably from fatigue or annoyance that no time limits had been announced for the event. At that hour, the remaining people were mostly serious collectors and a few others with no particular interest in the decorative arts but having an uncontrollable curiosity about other people's business: what they owned and what it was worth. These remaining participants had congregated around the tables of the four of us still available. I could see an old globe and a pair of brass andirons on the tables nearest me. A dozen people gathered in an irregular curve around my table.

A short, stocky man wearing a sport coat and tie was next in line. His stern manner suggested single-mindedness. Or perhaps he was irritated because of his long wait. He held a briefcase in one hand and in the other an object carefully wrapped in a cloth bag. I introduced myself and apologized for the wait.

"Are you qualified to appraise pewter?" he answered without any introduction. I said I described myself as a generalist, familiar with American pewter, and would be happy to go over his piece with him.

He stared at the cloth bag. "This is an important piece of pewter, and I don't want you to waste my time if you don't know what you're doing." His neck twitched slightly. I should have heeded the warning signs, but always curious, I encouraged him to have a seat and let me examine what he had brought in.

He unwrapped a pewter tankard, an American example made in the early nineteenth century, and holding it with both hands placed it carefully on the table, as though it were a delicate Fabergé egg. When I asked, he gave me permission to examine the tankard, essentially a lidded mug, often used to hold beer. Aware that he was testing my knowledge of pewter, I proceeded with caution. Fortunately, I had two reference works on American pewter with me.

After a few minutes of careful scrutiny, I said the mark on the base was clear and did not appear to have been altered: "Boardman & Hart" over "N. York," above an "X," I said, and added that this example was made in Connecticut after 1828.

Before I finished the sentence, the owner jumped in. "You're right about the mark, but you're wrong about where it was made. Why would it be marked New York if it was made somewhere else? I was born in New York." Hoping for patience, I continued, citing information I had found in one of my reference books. The Boardmans made pewter for several generations in Hartford, Connecticut, and when they opened a branch store in New York in 1828, they continued to manufacture their wares in Hartford but marked the pieces offered in New York with that mark. The man with the briefcase shook his head. "You're wrong."

Ignoring the issue of where it was made and knowing that my next comment would not be met with warmth, I gently suggested that at auction, I thought his tankard would carry an estimate of $300–$600. I pointed out that although pewter had been popular several years earlier, it, like the dry sinks in which pewter was often displayed, had faded in desirability in recent years.

With a quick gesture, he flipped open his briefcase and pulled out eight or ten dark brown folders. He opened one, handed me a formal written appraisal with a photo of his tankard, and said angrily that the tankard was worth $3,500. I read the appraisal and explained that the tankard might cost $3,500 to replace, if it were in good condition, but the handle of his tankard was badly repaired and might not even be original to the piece, adding that the appraisal did not mention this damage.

He pulled out more folders; he had been gathering appraisals of his tankard for several years and showed me articles on American pewter and photocopies of pages from price guides with pewter tankard entries highlighted in yellow. I read through the appraisals; values for his tankard ranged from $800 to $3,500, the one he first showed me. "You have found a lot of information," I remarked. "What do you want to know?"

Shaking his head as though tired of repeating himself, he complained wearily, "I want to know what the tankard is *really* worth."

"An appraisal is an opinion, and you have eight or ten opinions." I explained that insurance replacement appraisals such as his were what you would expect to pay if you were buying this tankard. "Real market value appraisals suggest what you could expect to realize if you were selling the tankard." I asked if he was planning on selling the tankard. He said no, he just wanted to know its real value.

One of the people watching and listening, a small older woman wearing a blue cardigan sweater, spoke up. "I'm a dealer, and I have several shelves of pewter in my shop, but no one ever looks at it." She smiled mischievously and, turning to the man, made an offer: "I'll sell you an eighteenth-century British tankard in great shape for fifty dollars."

The briefcase man glared at her. "My tankard is American, much more valuable than your British crap."

The blue sweater woman held her ground. "No one wants damaged pewter from any country."

Though I was exhausted and wanted the night to end, I plunged into the fray. "There is no real value. It is all pretend." I said that ideas we have about value are ascribed, culturally learned; they are not intrinsic to the piece. We make up numbers or ask others to make up numbers and call those numbers worth, or value.

I glanced at the briefcase man as I spoke. "What determines value is not age, provenance, auction records, price guides, or appraisals but rather how many people want to own it. If no one wants to own your pewter tankard, it really isn't worth anything except as a vessel to hold beer or dried flowers." I added that in some cultures, worth might be measured by utility, decoration, a line of descent, or durability and that in some preindustrial cultures, even gold and silver are not necessarily considered to be valuable.

"Well," he argued, "I live in this culture. Are you trying to tell me my tankard isn't worth anything?" He fingered the edges of the folders.

"No, I think you are after an absolute number, and there are no absolute numbers. Values change with time, place, and ideas about taste and fashion." He was after some sort of affirmation beyond his, or my, grasp.

The briefcase clicked shut, as all the brown folders were back in place. The blue sweater woman still smiled slightly to herself. I thanked the briefcase man for bringing in the pewter tankard and wished him well. He looked around and asked if I knew whether any of the other appraisers still at their tables knew anything about American pewter.

He was looking for someone who could validate the desire and expectation he felt when he looked at his Connecticut tankard, someone who saw what he saw. I did not. I wondered if it would have made any difference if I had said it was worth $6,000. It was the same damaged pewter tankard, important to him. Perhaps only him.

Suddenly, for the first time in many hours, there was no one standing at my table. I packed up my books and tools and walked away, stiff-legged and cramped, dropping the half-eaten plate of food in a large trash barrel, looking forward to a cold glass of beer when I got home, free from the fictions and seductions of ownership.

As I drove home, I considered the advantages of not owning anything, as ownership is often accompanied by burden and sadness, even anger. It takes effort and money to purchase, maintain, and insure possessions. If I bought nothing more to put in my house, I could use the money and time I saved for other pursuits. I might begin to understand my life and its possibilities in a different way, more open, less confined. I might be more inclined to support nonprofit agencies with values similar to mine or to visit the places where my ancestors once lived and worked. The next time I was with a person who seemed to be alone and afraid, I could sit with them and listen as they searched for words to define their anguish. I might learn to play the cello or begin a careful study of lichen. I might return to the Outer Hebrides, a place I had visited many times, and watch the ocean for a year or two and learn to be grateful.

For me, the most realistic understanding of ownership reflects the reality that it is an impermanent, transient experience, and in that regard, it is a myth.

PODIUM

I knew the address would take me to a large trailer park, but I was not deterred. I had found some remarkable pieces in humble dwellings. On my last visit to a trailer, I had looked at a fine painting, a very desirable New York snow scene by Guy Wiggins, though the owner declined to sell it as it had been a gift from an aunt. Today, this owner had said only that she had a rare box she might want to put in an auction.

Several weary potted geraniums rested on the front porch of her home, an older green camping trailer. An outdated women's bicycle with wide tires leaned against a tree. She met me at the door, a tall, thin woman with long arms and fingers. Though it was a mild sunny day in September 2002, she wore a wool cap and several layers of sweaters and aprons. She spoke rapidly with a slight accent I could not identify and looked to be in her mid-fifties. She invited me in, offering me a chair at her kitchen table; stale cooking odors lingered in the air.

She said she had tried unsuccessfully to figure out when and where her box had been made. She walked to the bedroom and returned with a small oval box, cupping it in front of her with both hands. After she laid it on the kitchen table, she said she had bought it at a church sale many years earlier and that several people had told her it was very rare.

The box was made of pan bone, thin slices of whale bone carefully decorated with scrimshaw hearts, flags, crosses, anchors, and other nautical symbols, and it was called a ditty box. I explained that it was probably created by a sailor in the mid-nineteenth century, perhaps given to a sweetheart when he arrived home after a long sea voyage. I noted that hers was a particularly nice example as it still had its original lid, and the decoration included a three-masted sailing ship flying a colorful American flag. She smiled occasionally and nodded as I spoke.

These boxes, I continued, were used to store a sailor's sewing implements: needles, thread, a punch to make holes in leather, a small pair of scissors—all necessary tools for a sailor's line of work. I explained that some of the most collectible ditty boxes were dated and would have included the names of the ship and the sailor who had made the box. As we talked, I glanced around the room looking for something else of value she might be willing to consign but saw nothing of note.

She asked why it was called a ditty box. I replied that I had sold several of these in the past and had read a number of explanations for the origin of the word "ditty." I said that to me, the most likely was that "ditty" had become a shortened version of the word "commodity": a commodity box. She asked how much it would sell for in one of my auctions. I said it would carry an estimate of $1,500–$2,500 but had the potential to do even better. She said immediately that she wanted me to sell the box for her, but before she signed the consignment agreement she wanted me to also sell some books.

She took me to the bedroom where four boxes of books were stacked on the bed. I emptied the boxes and saw immediately that the books had very little value, but I politely opened each one to look at titles and dates. Most appeared to be high school textbooks from the 1950s: geometry, English, biology, world history, home economics. A few were heavily used children's books—horses, pirates, hot air balloons, hunting in the Yukon—none rare or collectible. She watched carefully as I examined each book but made no comment.

"We have no market for these books," I told her quickly. She said she knew this but wanted me to take them along anyway. I tried again and repeated that the books had virtually no value; I knew of no one who would bid on them. I stressed that the ditty box was a jewel and would do well, but the books were simply not for us.

With her arms folded across her chest and her face slightly twisted, she replied, "If you don't take the books, I will keep the box." Other than convenience, was there any reason she wanted the books out of her house? As her decision did not seem to be negotiable, and rather than argue about it, I agreed to take the four boxes of books. I told her the ditty box would be pictured in the brochures for our next auction, and I would send her a copy when they were printed.

When auction day arrived, I met her during the preview, brochure in her hand, still wearing a wool cap against the cool November air, and welcomed her as we exchanged friendly greetings. During the auction, she sat near the back of the room and smiled a bit when her box came up. We had several phone and absentee bids on the ditty box, and bidding was spirited. Much to my delight, and I assumed the owner's delight, it brought over $5,000. I was also pleased when, later in the auction, the four boxes of books brought the extraordinary sum of $30.

How satisfying it is when all the elements of the auction process go well, I thought: a good, sellable object in excellent condition; a reasonable provenance; a good response to advertising; a strong selling price; and a happy client. No unforeseen event had hijacked our work with the ditty box: the owner had not changed her mind, no heirs or family members had appeared claiming that they were the owners of the box, and no one had suggested the box was a modern forgery, all problems I had experienced in the past with other clients.

When the auction was over, she came to the podium. I thanked her for her consignment and readied myself for at least modest praise for the high price we had achieved. Instead, she pointed at me, stabbing the air with an angry finger, and said abruptly, "You gave away my books," and walked quickly toward the doors of the auction gallery.

How foolish of me to have expected happiness.

Maybe the books were symbolic of an important era of her life, and no amount of money would have been enough for her. Perhaps she thought the higher value of the ditty box would elevate the bidding for the books. What had I missed? I will never know. I know that expecting praise for something I have done is a dead-end street. I need to find my own rewards—or better, not need rewards at all.

I smiled as I drove home after the auction and thanked myself for my conscientious work and for an excellent outcome in the sale of the ditty box.

····

At the end of another auction several months later, I had to deal with a different problem. By late afternoon, we had sold 764 lots, and the magic of yet another long auction day had worn off. I was weary. Most of the day had gone well, but very few auctions are without some errors: forgetting to advance an image on the monitors, losing track of who made the last bid. The most grievous error, however, is missing a bid.

We ask bidders to make their bids visible and obvious, but despite our vigilance, sometimes we fail to see a raised hand or gesture. Some are angry when this happens and take the mistake as a personal slight, a public act of personal rejection. Sometimes a bidder implies that we have purposefully not taken his or her bid. I've always wondered how it could possibly be in our best interest to not accept a bid.

On this occasion, I was prepared for the worst. The bidder had driven from St. Louis the previous day, in time to preview the auction. He was interested in art glass, and for this auction we had combined several collections including fine examples of Tiffany, Galle, Steuben, Daum, Baccarat, and other makers. During the preview he examined many pieces, and when I introduced myself, he said he dealt in fine art glass and also bought pieces for his own collection.

"You know, there is one piece I came for in particular, and it's the reason I drove all the way from St. Louis," he explained. I was curious about which piece it might be, but he didn't offer any further information, and I didn't ask. An auctioneer could use this sort of knowledge to a bidder's disadvantage.

He bid on many lots during the day and was successful on several, but near the end of the auction, I missed his bid on a large Steuben Blue Aurene bowl. He had moved around the room during the day, and when the Steuben bowl was offered, he was seated behind another bidder, partially obscured. As I said "Sold," he stood, waving his card in the air with wide sweeping semicircles. He was tall and muscular—and angry, I imagined, as he aired his frustration.

"I was bidding," he cried out. I apologized immediately and explained that I could not reopen the bidding once I said "Sold." He shook his head, pulled his card down, and bid no more. I then realized that the Steuben bowl might have been the piece he had referred to earlier, the prize for which he had driven so far.

As he approached the podium when the auction was over, I steadied myself for the predictable onslaught of retribution and wrath. Instead he extended his hand and said, "I just want to compliment you for a fine auction. It went very smoothly, and I really appreciate your efforts to write careful and detailed descriptions." He said that this was the first time he had attended one of our auctions and that he would be back again.

I could not have been more surprised. I waited for the "But..." I was sure would follow, but there was none. I was enormously relieved and apologized for missing his bid on the Steuben bowl. I told him I had expected dismay and resentment. His next words were, "Oh, I have the five-year rule. When I get angry over something, my rule is to wait five years before I tell the person off." He said his wife was killed in a car accident fourteen years earlier and that none of this buying, selling, and collecting was important enough to get upset about anyway.

CARPET

On a sunny September day in 2003, I knocked on the half-open door of a home in Montreat, a Presbyterian church, conference center, and neighborhood about ten miles east of Asheville. I had been told that the woman who lived here owned "a Windsor chair, some china, and a few other things" she might want to sell. Not a promising inventory, but whenever invited into a home, I went, the search for valuable objects always in play.

"Come on in, I don't get around very well," she hollered cheerfully.

Inside, she sat on a small rocking chair, her apron spread on her lap, and was using a pair of old black tailor's scissors to cut something into roughly equal pieces, each less than a foot square. It had been a finely woven prayer rug, its floral designs and rows of half diamonds now worn and faded. I thought it might be Turkish.

"I knew you wouldn't want this because it is so worn," she began. "I was cutting it into pieces to use for covering bricks. You know, they have great decorator colors and make good doorstop covers." She said she had read about this in a magazine.

I suggested gently that the rug might once have been quite valuable. She paused, the long, tapered blades of her scissors partway through a border in one corner. "Well, I had no idea," she exclaimed, putting down her scissors and smiling broadly through her large, irregular teeth. She said she had owned the rug for many years and had never paid much attention to it.

I explained that rugs of this quality were sometimes rewoven, and her rug might still have some value, even partially cut up. We could put all of it in a box and sell it in our next auction, if she was interested. She gathered the pieces into a conforming stack, smiled her toothy smile, and said that would be just fine. The box of rug pieces brought eighty dollars in our next auction, perhaps purchased by another doorstop enthusiast.

I have no memory of anything else in her home, but my encounter with her ill-fated rug was the first of several episodes in which a rug of some value appeared in an unlikely place and produced improbable results.

A steady stream of textiles had flowed through Brunk Auctions since we began our business in 1983, including the rugs of Persia, Turkey, Egypt, China, Russia, and England. Over time, we had offered Suzani embroideries, Navajo blankets, Greek bed coverings, French and Belgian tapestries, flat-woven kilims, Elizabethan needlework, tent panels, bag faces, saddle blankets, samplers, clothing, and costumes. Everything we offered was accompanied by a written description. Karen, our textile specialist, compiled catalog entries, but mostly by default I wrote the descriptions and condition reports for the rugs and carpets (larger rugs). An uneven stack and a tape measure awaited me before every auction.

I wanted our descriptions and photographs to be clear and accurate, to create trust in our work and in what we offered. I measured the carpets and counted the knots per square inch, often a measure of fineness. I noted wear and damage, reductions, color enhancers, rewoven areas. I could usually distinguish between older natural dyes and later commercial aniline dyes.

Yet I was rarely confident of the age and origin of older pieces, often the most important information for our catalogs. Was it a Heriz, or was it a Serapi, typically of more value, or possibly a rare Bakshaish? My biggest fear was that I would miss an important carpet and not advertise it properly. How gratifying it would have been to be able to write a description of a rare carpet and be specific to the period and place of its origin, describe the colors and the history of its design elements, and compare the piece to other known examples.

Several months later we were asked by the executor of a large estate to come with our truck and take whatever would do well at auction. On a hot June day, Fulton, Thomas, and two other staff traveled with me to eastern North Carolina. The porch of the large colonial-style house was bordered by a faithful row of square white columns. Inside, we were met with an invisible cloud of offensive odor, caused by pet urine. We often ran into stale, unpleasant air in unoccupied houses, but this was beyond anything in recent memory, the singe of ammonia with every breath. We opened windows and turned on the fans we always carried with us for these occasions.

We introduced ourselves to the executor, a friendly woman in her sixties wearing a Georgia sweatshirt and blue walking shoes, eager for us to take as much as possible from the house. We also met a young male bank employee, probably from the trust department, possibly overdressed for the occasion in his suit, vest, tie, glistening hair product, and polished shoes. He held a lengthy appraisal to which he frequently referred as we worked our way through the house.

In the living room, a row of six bronze urns rested on a fireplace mantel, which we were told held the ashes of six beloved dogs that had belonged to the late owner. I saw the engraved names on two of them as we walked by: Sarge and Major. We found about ten pieces of furniture suitable for our auctions and then checked the overgrown backyard to see if there were any lead figures, cast-iron chairs, fountains, or other sellable items but found nothing. In the driveway, we saw a dumpster standing at attention and beside it a stiff, reeking carpet, thrown to the ground in a pile, roasting in the sun, a familiar casualty in homes with pets. Urine contains salt and salt attracts moisture; combined, they attack the foundation of a carpet, which would eventually rot.

The carpet had scattered small holes, but by counting the knots, I could see that it was finely woven, over 200 knots per square inch, and once possibly of great value. I thought it might be a Tabriz carpet, similar to one we had recently sold for over $12,000. Or maybe it was a Kashan or an Ispahan.

Fulton looked at me, sensing what I was considering, and said, "No, don't even think about it. We are not going to put that mess on the truck. We can't hold our breath long enough." But I prevailed. After wrapping it in plastic and sealing it as best we could, Fulton and Thomas heaved it onto the back of the box truck and created a three-inch gap in the pull-down door to keep the air circulating around the mound of plastic.

When we reentered the house to finish our work, a carpenter was tearing up the oak floor in the dining room. The executor explained that the carpet in our truck had been in that room and the flooring had to be replaced.

Back home in Asheville, we slowly unfolded the rigid carpet onto heavy plastic in our large storage room, soaked both sides of the carpet with water, then cleaned and vacuumed both sides with a wet vacuum. We repeated this process at least twice a day for several weeks, with oversize exhaust fans ventilating the room. The carpet gradually became flexible and less repugnant and was now a candidate for restoration.

It would be sent to Turkey and be partially rewoven, treated with carefully chosen enzymes to neutralize the odor, and when finished, it would once again be a remarkable work of art. New yarn is chosen or created to match the warp, weft, and pile of the carpet and then dyed with natural dyes to match the original colors and their variations. The end fibers of the new yarn are then interwoven with the ends of the original yarn, so there is no visible change in texture or color.

I thought of a rug I had inherited several years earlier. I believe the rug is a Karabagh, though it also might be a Kuba or a Ladik, other types of Caucasian village rugs. It had been handed to my grandfather in 1921 by a farmer who lived in rural Turkey, near where my grandfather was working with a Mennonite relief agency helping distribute clothing and rebuild homes for Russian immigrants. The rug was a gift from a grateful homeowner, or so the family legend goes. It ended up in Virginia, where my aunt Mable had stored it for many years. When I picked up the rug in her attic, I saw strands of faded red and blue yarn in the nests the mice had constructed. My aunt recalled that as a child, she and my father had played with marbles on the rug, using the circular medallions as the borders for their games. The rug, now restored, rests in Nashville, Tennessee, on the floor in the home of my daughter, Ingrid, who will maintain the rug and its familial pedigree. Old rugs are always enhanced by a good story of origin.

Several months later, we were in a spacious home positioned at the edge of a golf course in Southern Pines, North Carolina; Ruby, our Asian specialist at the time, and two other staff were with me. The owners, a gracious elderly couple, were moving to a retirement community and were selling most of their possessions. The handsome two-story Gothic Revival structure was furnished with Asian art of varying age and value: porcelains, bronze statuary, lacquerware, hard stone carvings, coromandel screens, ivory figures. The gentleman explained that his parents had been in the diplomatic corps in China during the 1920s; he had inherited their collection. He walked with a gold-handled cane, which he used to point at specific objects as we moved through the house.

It took about two hours to list our inventory of consigned items as we surveyed the seven downstairs rooms. I asked if we could look around the upstairs. The lady of the house replied quietly, saying that we could take a look, but she was certain we would find nothing of value. She said this in a friendly way, smiling, a challenge of sorts. Without being too intrusive, we always made a point of opening every door and examining every dark, cluttered corner of a house to be sure we had not missed anything.

Upstairs, in the third guest bedroom, in a closet that discharged boxes and rolls of upholstery fabric when opened, we found a small, worn Chinese rug, about two by four feet and lacking pile—"thin," we would say. We saw only the dimmest vestiges of color, but a faint row of delicate waves was still visible in two of the borders.

Because of the soaring interest in Chinese decorative arts, we added the rug to our inventory and took it with us. I knew it was old, but, like the lady making doorstop covers, I didn't believe it could be of much value. I was wrong. In our catalog, based on the many photos I had examined, I described the rug as Chinese and guessed at the age. "Probably 19th century," I wrote, with an estimate of $600–$900. After it sold to a buyer in Europe for over $50,000, we learned that it was a rare Chinese survival of the sixteenth century. I still didn't know anything.

I had the instincts to be a scholar and the urge to immerse myself in the study of the many varieties of knots found in rugs to help me identify where and when they were woven. I longed for the time to begin such a study, but it would have to wait; I was working day and night to manage my expanding business. I had also learned that if I showed a rug to three knowledgeable rug enthusiasts, I might get three distinctly different opinions as to the origin of the rug. Rugs do not lend themselves to precise classifications. Or perhaps I was too impatient for sustained, systematic investigation, leaping erratically from one seductive detail of decorative arts history to the next.

. . . .

Several weeks later, on a rainy day in late February, we were working in a large Norfolk, Virginia, estate; our last day there. The three-story house contained only a fraction of the gentleman's far-ranging collection, scattered in eight locations. Part of a set of fine china in one house would match more of the same china in another location a mile away.

At most of these sites, we were met with disarray, unsavory conditions, and scant electricity; no site had running water. The floors of many rooms had a layer of debris, which had apparently been walked on for several years: magazines, cassette tapes, a disassembled air conditioner, food containers, clothing, furniture parts, rat feces, boxes on their sides spewing mildewed books.

Our crew of five was exhausted and grimy, weary of trying to make order out of chaos and tired of rigging up portable lights to see what we were doing. But our work was rewarded with good, sellable auction pieces: marble busts and bronzes, eighteenth- and nineteenth-century American and European furniture, porcelains, architectural accessories, and over 100 paintings, some by well-known artists.

Behind the house slept an old double garage with heavy wooden doors that skidded open from the center—the last storage facility to be checked for possible auction candidates. The interior was dark and clammy; rows of wooden fire surrounds salvaged from old houses had been stacked in tight rows and were covered with a haze of spiderwebs and dead insects.

We loaded two or three of the better surrounds on the truck and looked around, hoping that we were finally finished. Near the door to one side were a large, misshapen cardboard box and a black plastic garbage bag. The box contained a rotting Aubusson tapestry, too damaged to even consider for restoration; the garbage bag held a large, old carpet. I held one corner while we unrolled three or four feet. It looked promising, so we loaded it on the back of the truck and finally headed home.

In Asheville, a week later, we unrolled the carpet and found that it was in remarkable condition, with only a few of the usual repairs and threadbare areas often seen in older carpets. The colors were exceptional: rich blues and ambers, the red of worn brick. In the corners, I saw repeating tulip-like flowers finely woven in five colors on a white background.

It lay comfortably in one of our galleries for several months. Occasionally, a rug buyer would come by to preview our next auction, and I would show him or her the carpet, hoping for a definitive identification. Their reaction was usually puzzlement; all found the carpet attractive, but no one had seen any similar examples upon which to base an attribution. Several countries of origin were suggested: Persia, Spain, Turkey, Russia. One person speculated that it had been rolled up or otherwise protected for many years as there was very little visible fading from excessive exposure to light. A gentleman from New York, whose opinion I respected, knelt on the floor to examine the carpet, turning over corners and rubbing the pile and assessing the quality of the wool, the warp and weft, the variety of knot, and the selvage and fringe. "This may be an important carpet," he whispered, half to himself. I asked where he thought it was from. He suggested Turkey.

I listened and watched as more people inspected the carpet, a few taking photos with their cell phones, not yet a common practice in 2003. Others made phone calls, describing the carpet in detail to colleagues or potential buyers. I gradually understood this was not an ordinary floor covering.

We described the carpet in our printed and online catalogs as Turkish, possibly eighteenth-century, with an estimate of $5,000–$10,000. As usual, I was guessing at the date. People began calling, making appointments to see the carpet, asking for detailed photos. Many buyers we had never met came to examine it, most not offering any information that might elevate interest in it and increase competition when it was sold. Carpet collectors and dealers from Europe and several cities in the United States flew in or sent agents to evaluate it, all propelled by the possibility that a carpet of such age and beauty even existed. Buyers reserved phones and sent reassuring letters of credit from their banks, and by the week of the auction, it was clear that the carpet was going to do very well.

We exhibited the carpet on a row of eight-foot tables so it could be examined more easily and to prevent foot traffic. During the preview, I spoke with a dealer and friend from California who had followed our auctions for several years, occasionally buying a rug or two. He stood beside the carpet, his arms folded across his chest, his face weak with despair. "I have no hope of owning this carpet," he murmured quietly. "I came just to see it. It is more beautiful than I ever imagined."

We offered the carpet on May 31, 2003. The gallery was crowded, many people sitting or standing at the back of the room, staking out territory from which they could easily be seen when bidding. Some glanced around, assessing their competition, checking how many phones were available for phone bidding. Others huddled in small groups, perhaps seeking agreements by which they would not to bid against each other on a particular item.

An irregular ring of people surrounded the tables displaying the carpet. One man, frowning, flipped over a corner of it, then turned to a companion, shaking his head in obvious disapproval of some sort—nothing to betray interest, but his very presence, of course, suggesting otherwise. One man approached me and asked to speak with me in private. We backed up a couple of steps as he explained his proposal. He was interested in buying the carpet and wanted me to understand his signals: when he was sitting down, he was bidding, and when he was standing up, he was not bidding; he hoped this strategy would mask his bidding to his competition. I told him that this was not a service we could provide and he would need to bid with his bid card.

The carpet was lot fifty-seven and came up about an hour into the auction. When I asked for an opening bid of $5,000, fifteen or twenty bidders in the gallery raised their hands or bid cards, and several phone bidders also responded. A short, animated man, far to one side of the crowd, his face flushed in shades of anxiety, yelled, "$50,000." I asked for $55,000, but no one lowered their hand. The bidding rose steadily in $5,000 increments to $100,000, several bidders slowing dropping out. My friend from California kept his hand in the air to about $80,000 but was soon swept away by the determination of other bidders. He smiled and waved at me slightly from the back of the room as he pulled his hand down.

When the bidding reached $100,000, I switched to $10,000 increments. By the time the selling price had risen to $160,000, only two bidders were still active, one a phone bidder, the other Moshe Tabibnia, who had traveled to Asheville from Milan, Italy, to buy the carpet. He believed it was made in the sixteenth century and was the prototype, the pinnacle of design and artistry, for carpets from Karapinar, a small village in Turkey, and the model for carpets woven in that region in the centuries that followed.

After a committed battle with the phone bidder, Tabibnia bought the carpet for $297,000, $270,000 plus 10 percent buyer's premium. He had bought fine carpets from us before, so I was confident it was a solid sale. The room burst into applause.

News of the carpet's sale was carried in Chicago, New York, and Los Angeles newspapers. In London, *Hali*, the preeminent magazine of carpets, textiles, and Islamic art, carried an article written by a carpet aficionado who traveled south from New York to the small mountain town of Asheville, hoping to buy the carpet for $100,000 or less. He thought there might be a bargain in such a rural setting, but when he arrived, he found many well-informed buyers from distant locales, including several of international reputation.

Several years later, Moshe Tabibnia published a large, finely illustrated slipcase book, *Milestones in the History of Carpets* (Milan, September 2006), accompanying an exhibition by the same name. Vivid color details of the carpet we sold decorate the covers of the book and slipcase. A lengthy, scholarly description of the carpet written by Dr. Jon Thompson, an Oxford University textile historian, begins with these words:

> A central Anatolian carpet with three gently lobed medallions with pendants on a blue-green ground alternating with white-ground half and quarter medallions.
>
>   Woolen pile on a woolen foundation, 629 × 221 cm. (20.63 × 7.25 ft.)
>   The appearance of this carpet in 2003 is truly a milestone in the history of carpets. Far surpassing in grandeur and condition its

nearest rival, the fragmentary Bernheimer piece. This hitherto unknown Karapinar carpet has extraordinary visual appeal and ranks among the great finds of recent times. It appears to be the oldest and best example yet known of a group of carpets about which there is still much to learn. Evidence for dating is based on the observation that its décor derives from the two Ottoman court styles current in the second half of the sixteenth century. (p. 226)

At last, an accurate description worthy of a fine carpet, and what an honor, fortuitous as it was, for me to have participated in the discovery of this remarkable survival, from complete anonymity in a garbage bag to uncommon fame in the world of fine and rare old carpets.

In a review of Moshe Tabibnia's book, published in the London-based *Financial Times* (October 28–29, 2006), the reviewer described Tabibnia's participation in the auction the day the carpet was sold and Tabibnia's assessment that the carpet's wool "felt like cashmere." The writer also suggested that the size of the carpet, about twenty by seven feet, was "far beyond the dimensions of an ordinary village house" and that "the only building in Karapinar in the late 1500s that would have required, and demanded, such finery was the new mosque."

If this assessment is correct, and the carpet spent much of its life in the relative safety of a mosque, that might account for its excellent condition, given Islamic beliefs and rituals to ensure cleanliness in mosques, including the removal of shoes when praying.

As I write these words, I try to imagine the area around Karapinar, a small, dusty village about an hour's drive east of Konya in central Turkey and an important stop on the network of trade routes known as the Silk Road, linking China and Europe for 1,500 years.

Who were the people who had a part in the creation of this carpet, and how had it intersected their lives: those who raised the sheep and gathered, cleaned, carded, and twisted the wool into thread; those who had collected the materials to create the dyes for the yarn; those women who had strung the warp and weft of the carpet, its foundation, and who had tied the many thousands of knots? Did they talk about the carpet as they worked? What did they say? Was a particular person responsible for the design of the carpet, or was it woven from the collective memories of other similar carpets and tapestries?

If the carpet was intended for their mosque in Karapinar, the women who wove it were, in one limited sense, doing it for themselves; they and their families would have sat and prayed on the carpet, separated by gender. Those women may have understood its beauty in ways not accessible to most of us, twenty-first-century travelers with little tactile or instinctive connection to the details of the carpet's construction to inform our understanding of their work.

For me, these mysteries are a central component of the carpet's beauty. Silent and confident, it sustains the secrets of its making and the texture of the cultural landscape from which it emerged. Perhaps the existence of the carpet, the aesthetic and historic statement it makes, is enough, a sufficient testimony.

What an honor to have lived with this remarkable carpet for several months, to imagine the making of it, and to consider its survival through an epic 450-year journey. I think of the people who created this work of art, who tied these thousands of knots. I want them to know that its transcendent beauty has only grown since they held it in their hands.

FOREST

We entered through a back door that opened into the kitchen. The floor was covered with debris—broken glass, newspapers, food containers, bags of garbage, old telephone books, clothing, shoes, a broken electric can opener—all crunching under our feet as we picked our way across the rubble. The woman showing us through the house warned us not to open any of the three refrigerators, as she felt they might be the source of the strong odor that had greeted us. She needn't have worried; there was no chance we would touch a refrigerator. We went back to our truck to put on masks and retrieved a flat shovel to clear some of the broken glass.

On this fall day in 2001, we were in Ocala, Florida, with a crew of six and two large rental trucks. The blurry photographs we had been sent promised stained glass lamps, painted furniture, samplers, stacks of Shaker pantry boxes, Staffordshire figures, and rooms of eighteenth- and nineteenth-century American furniture. When we drove up to the 1950s split-level brick house, we saw hibiscus and sprawling night-blooming cereus scattered in the unkempt yard.

Most of the house was inaccessible. Furniture, boxes, lamps, bookcases, and fully loaded china cabinets were stacked against doors and had to be emptied and moved to gain entrance to adjoining rooms. Despite the terrible state of the house, we saw enough furniture and decorations to justify sorting through the wreckage; we had driven our two large trucks twelve hours and wanted to take back enough merchandise to at least cover the cost of meals and lodging for six people and the truck rentals. Sometimes, we lost money on these long-distance adventures. As I looked around the house, I saw that this one could well be a loser.

After exploring what we could of the first floor, I approached the stairs to the upper level, which contained three bedrooms and a bath. The woman showing us through the house, the executor of the estate, stopped me and said we didn't need to go upstairs, there was nothing there for us: a family member was living in two of the rooms, but he was away at work during the day. I could not imagine anyone living in this place.

The owner of the property, a woman, was deceased, and the executor told us to take what we could sell and dispose of the rest. We ordered a fifteen-foot dumpster, which was promptly delivered and parked in the driveway. We decided to avoid the kitchen and begin at the front of the house. After half an hour of moving furniture and restacking leaning piles from the inside, we were able to open the front door and begin our work. Two people filled five-gallon buckets, and two others ran relays to the dumpster to empty them; we sorted through broken dishes, old clothing, used tissues, pillows whose foam rubber cushions had turned to sticky yellow powder. A rubber toy had melted into a scaly, shapeless mass and was stuck to a glass surface.

But our efforts eventually yielded sellable merchandise: a laminated rosewood sofa, a fine Russian samovar, art deco floor lamps, and the samplers and Shaker-style boxes seen in the earlier photographs. By noon of the first day, we had worked our way through half of the living room, but the prospect of lunch presented new problems. We were far too dirty to present ourselves at any restaurant, but there was nowhere in or near the house we could sit to eat; we couldn't imagine getting clean enough to hold any food in our hands. Finally, we sent someone to get takeout food. He brought back lunch, rolls of clean paper towels, and great quantities of disinfectant. The cleanest places we could find were our own trucks, where we ate with doors and windows open to reduce the midday heat. When we needed restrooms, we drove to the nearest McDonald's.

After lunch, one of our crew, Bill, went out to the backyard and opened a small storage building. He found a four-drawer walnut chest that looked promising and called us over to take a look. He had trouble opening the first drawer, which was stuck in the humid air, but with a sustained pull, it finally flew open. Out jumped a wharf rat the size of a small possum. Bill let out a shriek and jumped back, shaking his hands as though they had been defiled. The rat lumbered across the yard and ran to the top of a nearby palm tree. Then we noticed that the top of every palm tree in the yard had a cluster of rats huddled at the top.

We gradually accepted that we were working in the company of many rats and slowly made our way back into the house. The men and women of my crew, all veterans of dirty houses and difficult work, began several sentences with "How could anyone possibly . . . ?" and "Why didn't they ever . . . ?," but soon we were all at work again.

Later that afternoon, while I was attempting to remove two large gilt-framed mirrors from the walls flanking the stairway to the upper level, my foot touched the top step, which squeaked a bit. This triggered a rampage of barks and snarls from the two occupied rooms. Fulton said quickly, "Dobermans." I backed off the top step, and the angry outburst subsided. When I stepped up again, the dogs were again enraged; the doors shook as they threw themselves against them. I shined a flashlight down the hall and saw claws and teeth scratching and chewing at the base of the doors, rounded from repeated attacks by the dogs. Once the mirrors were down and we got off the squeaking top step, we heard no more.

It was easy to be preoccupied with the unsavoriness of our work, but viewed from the perspective of the deceased person in whose home we were now working, what we were doing was also very intrusive. Under no circumstances would the owner have desired or imagined a dumpster and two large trucks parked in her yard and six people digging through her house. In later years, the staff and I remembered this trip to Ocala by the unusual details—the refrigerators, the jumping rat—but we also remember the sadness of it all.

We often encountered the slowly collapsing lives of older people, many of whom lived alone. They were often dealing with a gradually shrinking living space as their strength and mobility waned, decreased contact with caring people or agencies, rows of prescription medicines on dressers and kitchen tables, and a loss of will to attempt even the simplest improvement in their lives: aging creatures seeking refuge in the forest of their own homes.

I imagined a conversation with the owner of this house, she who had been unable to throw away a drugstore advertisement from 1956 or the plastic holder that gripped six cans of Diet Coke ten years ago. She who could not sort or rank what surrounded her. Would I seek an explanation, or could I, without judgment, allow her to be as she was, in this dense underbrush of trash? Maybe it was not hers. Maybe she did not see it, the accumulation having arisen of its own accord, a slow, unnoticed growth around her.

Perhaps she had early symptoms of dementia, her world blurring in and out of focus. Or multiple sclerosis, her slightest exertion inviting exhaustion.

Maybe she felt safer when she was surrounded by what she had saved, none of it seen as trash, some of it reminders of happier times.

As was often the case when working with older clients, I tried to picture my own situation when I was older and possibly facing chronic illness. I was sixty-one years old on this trip to Ocala and assumed I was years away from such challenges, but of course I had no idea what my health would be and what adaptations I might need to make in later years.

Our work lasted three days; the dumpster was emptied and returned twice. Our trucks were both full, the downstairs of the house now largely empty. The refrigerators stood as we had found them, now solitary monuments in a curated interior landscape.

We returned to Asheville and over the next several weeks prepared what we brought back for the next auction. All surfaces were cleaned and all glass surfaces were polished; large pieces were turned upside down, thoroughly vacuumed, disinfected, and cleaned of cobwebs and dirt. When we set up the auction preview, the pieces from Ocala were blended with fine paintings, silver, and Oriental rugs from other estates. In our carpeted galleries, with track lighting playing on reflective surfaces, the pieces looked as good as we could make them.

During the preview the day before the auction, a well-dressed woman approached me with many compliments for our presentation. She was standing beside the rosewood sofa from Ocala, her hand resting on the crest rail, her pendant earrings sparkling a bit. "I can't imagine the grand homes you are invited to explore. What a rare treat it must be for you and your staff to go through these estates. I know there is a lot to do with all the photography and advertising you do, but I can't imagine how exciting it must be, just taking these things off the walls and bringing them here." She said she had been coming to our auctions for several years and that she would love to work for me. "If you ever have any openings," she added, "please give me a call. I'm an interior decorator and have a lot of experience setting up displays." I thanked her for her kind words.

TABLE

In 2003, Hickory Museum of Art, in Hickory, North Carolina, deaccessioned a large group of objects and asked if we would offer them at auction. Hickory Museum's purpose is to collect and exhibit American art, and its deaccessioned pieces were not related to this goal; some of the material was from a group of weapons collected in Malaysia during World War II. Property deaccessioned by museums was always intriguing, so we headed to Hickory, about seventy-five miles east of Asheville.

When we arrived, the director of the museum led two of my staff and me to a large storage room. Several tables were covered with rows of kris—daggers and short swords with wavy blades, many with ornate horn mounts. We took these, a few Chinese porcelains, and a group of African carvings and weapons. In one corner of the room, I noticed a fine micro-mosaic table, which I knew had considerable value. I asked if it was available to be auctioned. Yes, it was available, but it had been appraised for $7,500, and we could take it for auction only if we guaranteed it would bring at least $5,000. I quickly agreed to a reserve of $5,000, delighted that we had an exceptional piece to offer from the collection. We completed the consignment agreement and loaded the heavy, two-piece table on our truck.

The museum had documentation indicating the table had been given to them in 1949 by Adolph Levitt, owner of the Doughnut Corporation of America, which later became Krispy Kreme Doughnuts. The museum had opened its doors five years earlier, in 1944. What a curious combination, I mused, doughnuts and a neoclassical table. There must be a good story here, some remarkable yarn I could unravel.

In the past, we had sold several small, framed micro-mosaic wall panels, usually depicting famous Greek and Roman structures, but nothing of this magnitude; the micro-mosaic top of the table measured 51¾ inches by 26¾ inches. It was created by assembling tens of thousands of tiny glass tesserae (thin rods or canes) stacked on end to create an elaborate classical composition: a central medallion circled with a wreath of ivy, spirals of vines and flowers, masks, and a double Greek key border. We found very few auction records for similar micro-mosaic tables, but our research led us to believe the top had been made by Giacomo Raffaelli, an Italian artist who lived 1753–1836, and that two similar examples of his work were held by the Hermitage Museum, St. Petersburg, Russia, and by the Pitti Palace, Florence, Italy. Raffaelli is considered to be the finest micro-mosaic artist of that era.

In our catalog description of the table and in my discussion with prospective bidders, I stressed the rarity and the fine detail of the micro-mosaic top and gave less attention to the wooden base, which was not fitted or attached to the top. At some point, the ebonized portions of the base had been painted white, but the gilt highlights had thankfully been spared.

In general, the top of a table with a base of different origin would be called a "marriage." An unmatched base usually devalues the piece, not unlike putting a bookcase on top of a desk by another maker and calling it a secretary. In our catalog, we pictured the complete table and a detail of the top. I cataloged the base as "later," meaning that in our opinion, the top and the base were not made at the same time. This turned out to be true, but the base held other surprises.

Many people examined the table in the weeks prior to the auction. One gentleman called and asked about the base in some detail and, after hearing my comments, made a strange request. Since the base and the top probably had different origins, and the value of the table was primarily the top, could he purchase the base for $10,000, before the auction? He pointed out that this would only add to the money the piece would fetch since the top was the rare and extraordinary part. I told him I would consider his offer and let him know in a few days. I tried to find other similar bases in case I had missed something, which of course I had.

We featured the micro-mosaic top of the table on the cover of our color brochure for the auction and mailed it to several thousand individuals, shops, and galleries. This and our other advertising had produced many inquiries about the table, and my instinct was to sell the top and base together, as a single unit. When I called the next day to turn down the gentleman's offer, he restated his arguments and suggested I was throwing away "found money" for my client, but I didn't change my mind. I knew it was a rare table, and I was confident it would do well. I also knew how difficult it would be to sell the top without the base. I didn't mention it, of course, but compared to the remarkable, finely detailed, colorful top, the base to me seemed heavy, and despite its good proportions it duplicated few if any of the refined elements of the top.

Almost all the seats in our gallery were occupied when we offered the table in our September 2003 auction, with an intentionally low estimate of $5,000–$10,000. Low estimates often encourage bidding. During the preview, many people had put their name on a chair, defining their territory. Others stood at the back of the room, to make sure their bids were not missed. Four or five staff members were standing with phone bidders, and several people had left absentee bids. The room was quiet, the excitement palpable, a sheet of ice about to crack. A woman sitting in the front row, who had been reading for the past hour, put her magazine down and pulled a bid card from her purse.

I was poised and eager and wondered if this event would provide a moment of high drama, perhaps a welcome affirmation of our work. All the principal elements in this narrative had converged: the visions and skill of Giacomo Raffaelli, the intercontinental journey of the table that now rested in front of everyone, our investigation into its construction and history, the museum's hopes for a substantial return, and the bidding strategies planned by many people. All these veins of energy had now joined for this eruption of sound and gesture, which would last less than five minutes. What would Raffaelli have thought had he been sitting in the crowd that morning? Other than his micro-mosaic tabletop, he would have noticed only scattered elements of neoclassical architecture and design in the pieces we were selling that day.

I asked for an opening bid of $10,000, and eight or ten bid cards went up, including that of the woman on the front row. A man standing in the back yelled out, "$30,000." This is known as a takeout bid, jumping the bid in an attempt to scare off others. But it works only if the jump is substantially higher than expectations. His $30,000 bid intimidated no one. The bidding sailed along quickly, with bids coming from all quarters. The woman in the front row held her card high in the air. Many bidders take their cards down after each bid to consider each bid or to slow down the bidding, but her card never moved. She said something to a companion beside her and never looked at the table or at me, as if to say, "Let me know when we are finished."

The people across the back of the room, several of whom had flown in from New York and at least two from Europe, quickly realized that she stood between them and ownership of the table. Several tried unsuccessfully to dislodge her apparent resolve. When her bid was $150,000, one gentleman shouted, "$200,000." A second later, I took her bid at $210,000, at which point he shook his head angrily and sat down. At $300,000, there were only two bidders, one on the phone and the lady in the front row. She finally prevailed at $440,000, and the room broke into applause. She walked quickly to the cashier's desk, finalized her payment arrangements, and departed. The sale of the table was over, and we had 800 more lots to sell.

I called the director of the Hickory Museum that evening to tell her what the table had brought. Astonished and joyous, she declared that that income would secure the museum's finances for several years.

The table was purchased by a European buyer, the woman in the front row presumably bidding on his behalf. We soon learned that the base of the table had been designed by Thomas Hope, the well-known English neoclassical designer of the early nineteenth century, and was an important example of his work. Hope had designed the base specifically for the micro-mosaic top, which he may have purchased in Rome in 1795. I never learned the identity of the man who had offered $10,000 for the base, but I would soon understand why he had tried.

Sometime later, Carlton Hobbs, a dealer in fine antiques in New York, bought the table and published a lavishly illustrated scholarly volume, *The Thomas Hope Table: A Rediscovered Masterpiece* (New York: Carlton Hobbs, 2007).

In March 2008, the table reappeared in an exhibit of Thomas Hope's work at the Victoria and Albert Museum, London, and later that year at the Bard Graduate Center, New York, the catalog for the exhibition titled *Thomas Hope: Regency Designer*. It included scholarly articles describing Hope's designs for neoclassical interiors and furniture and the social and historical context in which he worked. The catalog's description of the table was accompanied by a photograph after conservation, the white paint removed from the base to reveal its original ebonized surface and fine gilt details. The ends of the table were inspired by Roman and Etruscan thrones and sarcophagi, themselves derived from Athenian vases of the sixth century BC (*Thomas Hope: Regency Designer* [New York: Bard Graduate Center for Studies in the Decorative Arts, Design, and Culture, 2008], 396–97). The base didn't seem as heavy to me now.

I found reoccurring pleasure when something we had sold turned out to be an important object and did well at auction. I wished, of course, that I had recognized the work of Thomas Hope from the beginning, but reading through scholarly descriptions of historically significant examples of decorative arts, after we had sold them, was equally gratifying. My chief responsibility was to get information about important pieces in front of relevant dealers, museums, and collectors prior to the auction. In this case, I was pleased that we had correctly identified the maker of the micro-mosaic top.

The fact that Thomas Hope had designed the base of the table was a significant element in the table's desirability. Hope (1769–1831) was a patron of the arts; he and others in his family were Dutch bankers of great wealth who had moved to London in 1794. Thomas Hope's brother Henry Philip Hope collected precious gems, including the well-known Hope Diamond. In 1799, Thomas Hope bought a house on Duchess Street in London, built in the 1770s by the architect Robert Adam, who, like Hope, designed interiors and furniture in the neoclassical style.

Thomas Hope was a passionate collector of paintings and a wide range of modern and antique works of art. About 1800, he built a ninety-six-by-twenty-four-foot "Picture Gallery" as part of his expansion of the Duchess Street mansion to display some of his vast collection, and his drawings of that gallery included our micro-mosaic table. End and side views of the table also appear in Hope's book, *Household Furniture*, published in 1807. The cover of the Carlton Hobbs book features a watercolor of the Picture Gallery at Duchess Street, the micro-mosaic table in prominent view. At the time of this writing, I obtained a copy of Hobbs's book and became reacquainted with the remarkable classical details of the table and the history of its construction.

In 1807, Hope also purchased a classical mansion in Surrey known as Deepdene, which he transformed into a second showcase for his tastes in architecture, painting, and sculpture. Sometime after 1824, the micro-mosaic table was moved to Deepdene, where it resided in the Etruscan Room, a room created for the display of classical vases. When Thomas Hope died in 1831, Deepdene was rebuilt into an Italian villa by Hope's son Henry Thomas Hope.

In 1917, the contents of Deepdene, including the Etruscan Room and the micro-mosaic table, were sold at an auction conducted by Humbert and Flint; the table brought £101, a considerable sum at the time. In 1851, the Duchess Street mansion was sold for demolition, though many drawings of it survive. Deepdene was demolished in 1969 and replaced by an office building, after having provided offices for the British Railway until 1966. Both houses expanded by Thomas Hope, their interiors so carefully designed to display his thoughtfully chosen objects, were eventually demolished.

How frail, I thought, these grand structures seem to have been, symbols of wealth and ambition; how fleeting the experience of ownership.

The following is a description of the top of the table from the 1917 Humbert and Flint auction, in typical slightly pompous English decorative art dialect.

> The rectangular top, of micro-mosaic, centered by a rondel containing a krater-form vase against a sky-blue ground, surrounded by a complex system of polychrome acanthine decoration on a white field with classical masks *en grisaille* and geometric framed vignettes each containing a study *en grisaille* of an agonistic vase set against a dark blue ground, the central field enclosed in a complex illusionistic greek-key [*sic*] pattern with dark blue border, the outer edge and face of *rosso antico* marble. The underside with various markings . . .

Adolf Levitt, "The Donut King" (1883–1953), immigrated to the United States in 1890 with his family, Russian refugees, settling originally in Milwaukee, Wisconsin. In 1920, while owning a chain of bakeries in New York, Levitt invented a donut-making machine (he had changed the spelling of "doughnut") and eventually became a very wealthy man.

From the 1917 auction of the contents of Deepdene, to 1949, when Adolf Levitt donated the table to the Hickory Museum of Art, the whereabouts of the table are unknown, though we do know that for some unknown reason, the white paint on portions of the base was added after the 1917 auction.

Production of Krispy Kreme donuts began in 1937, in Winston-Salem, North Carolina, where Krispy Kreme corporate headquarters is still located. In the early years, the popular donuts were made in an abandoned warehouse in Old Salem. How or when Adolph Levitt came to own the table is unknown. Perhaps he bought it during the Depression.

Other than the museum being located seventy miles west of Winston-Salem, I can find no connection between the Hickory Museum of Art and Adolf Levitt, who died in 1953. His obituary, published in the *New York Times*, October 39, 1953, describes his success as a confident entrepreneur, but all the charities listed are Jewish agencies and hospitals; there is no sign of any interest in fine arts, museums, classical furniture, or late eighteenth-century tables.

PAINTING

In the mid-1990s, on late Friday afternoons, I frequently found myself in Chan Gordon's bookstore on Page Avenue in downtown Asheville, often with Bill Hart, who had just finished an essay on the photographer George Masa, and Mark Rosenstein, owner of the Market Place, a fine restaurant several blocks away. On any given occasion, our discussions might include mention of a Johnathan Williams tale, Greg Maddux, Michael Ondaatje, a loose thread of local history, or the merits of the single malt Scotch we were all enjoying.

Chan, with his wife, Miegan, owned the Captain's Bookshelf, specializing in fine and rare books. He was one of the reasons my antiques and auction business made it past a struggling one-person adventure. A native of Asheville, he was familiar with many of the great homes in the area. When heirs or descendants were confronted with the task of dealing with a large house full of personal property, they often called Chan because, as they said, "We don't know what to do with the books." Chan would often recommend me to these clients as someone who could help with their paintings, silver, furniture, and the like; several substantial consignments followed.

One evening, after the others had left, Chan described to me an important painting that had been in a local home for four generations. He said it depicted the village of Asheville and was painted in 1850 by the well-known African American artist Robert Duncanson. Chan knew I was always looking for exceptional things to sell and quickly emphasized that the sale of the painting was not being considered but that he could probably arrange for me to see it someday.

A year or two later, I began work on an anthology we were planning to publish on the history and cultures of Western North Carolina. I had seen many fine examples of the material culture of the region pass through our auctions and realized that much of this—the ceramics, textiles, woodworking, architecture, photography, products of the Arts and Crafts movement, and a glorious array of folk art—was largely undocumented. I decided to hire local writers and scholars to remedy this deficiency and publish their work.

By this time, I knew the owner of the painting was Mary Parker, a fourth-generation descendant of James Patton, who had emigrated from Ireland in 1790. The painting was in her home on Charlotte Street in Asheville. I had not seen the painting, but from Chan's description, I thought a photo of it would make an excellent cover for our book. I asked Chan if he could arrange a meeting with Mary Parker so I could see this rare work of art and discuss the book.

Several days later, I visited Mary Parker with Jerry Israel, a mutual old friend. Her stately two-story white house had been added to and modified many times since her grandfather Thomas Walton Patton built the house in 1869. Several years earlier, in September 1861, on land just east of where the Patton house was later built, the Twenty-Ninth Infantry Regiment of the Confederate army was organized. The place was known as Camp Patton.

Mary greeted us warmly and led us into the dining room. "Well!" she exclaimed, pointing at the Duncanson depiction of Asheville hanging above a sideboard. "There is the painting, and those people in the foreground looking down at the village are some of my family." She began almost every sentence with an enthusiastic "Well!" and a slight downward nod of her head.

Mary, Jerry, and I sat at the dining room table while Mary discussed her family and pieces of special interest in the room, her comments always kind and gracious. "My sister Josie gave me this vase years ago, and I have no idea what it is, but I think it is perfectly lovely." She said that most of the silver on the sideboard was from Charleston and belonged to Henrietta Kerr, one of her great-grandmothers. Each piece in the room was a familiar keepsake resting in a predictable location, markers with which she could confirm for herself where she was in time and place.

Mary spoke at length about the painting, which had never been out of her family, and how its history wrapped around several of her ancestors and the town of Asheville. How Duncanson and James Washington Patton, Mary's great-grandfather, came to know each other and arrange for the painting to belong to Patton was unknown. Patton may have commissioned Duncanson to paint the scene.

I explained that my son, Andrew, a graduate student in the Winterthur Program in Early American Culture, Winterthur, Delaware, would be honored to do a thorough study of the painting, since it had never been published. I had told Andrew about the painting several times, which had led to discussions of his writing an essay and the possibility, however remote, of us selling the painting one day. I told Mary his essay would be included in the book we were planning. I suggested that a photo of it would be an extraordinary cover for a collection of essays and research on Western North Carolina. Mary said she would be delighted to have Andrew write about the painting. When I relayed this to Andrew a few days later, he was honored to take on the project.

Chan was right: it was a rare and exceptional painting, connecting regional and local history to the broader field of nineteenth-century American art. It portrayed a cluster of buildings in the center of the village with clear depictions of the Presbyterian church, the jail, and Ravenscroft School, a building that still stands. Mount Pisgah was the highest peak in the distant mountain range.

Nineteenth-century landscapes of Southern cities are rare enough, but this painting was the oldest known of the tiny village of Asheville. The date, 1850, and Duncanson's signature were clearly visible on the back of the canvas. He was the first African American artist to achieve wide acclaim, nationally and internationally.

In the following months, Jerry and I visited Mary Parker several times, as she had asked us to sell some of her Charleston silver. When she wanted us to come over and look at things, Mary would write a courteous letter, asking me to come by if it was not too inconvenient.

Mary was something of a legend in Asheville for her support of many organizations and of people running for public office. She made her political views known to all and at age eighty-nine had no fear of anyone. I enjoyed her descriptions of herself. She said she was a bleeding-heart liberal since birth, a "yellow dog Democrat," and would vote for the Democrat even if it was a yellow dog. She was also one of the few people I had ever met who thought it was appropriate to pay taxes. She said that she and her siblings had "fed at the public trough" when they got their educations and that she was happy to be able to give back "some of that expense."

I decided to help Andrew with his research by seeing if I could find any local record of the painting. Several days later, I was in Pack Memorial Library to look through all the microfilmed copies of the *Asheville Messenger*, the local newspaper in 1850, looking for any possible mention of Duncanson to verify his presence in Asheville. But I found only four microfilm copies of the *Asheville Messenger* for the entire year of 1850. I went through the four copies, contemplating the slim odds of finding any mention of Duncanson. But in the bottom right corner of the last column of the last issue, dated August 14, 1850, I struck gold: "Artists Mr. R. S. Duncanson and Mr. A. O. Moore, of Cincinnati, Ohio, have been at our village for a fortnight or more, taking sketches of the mountain and river scenery." There it was in black and white, a record of Duncanson in Asheville in 1850. I let out a loud cheer when I read this in the library and called Andrew immediately with the good news. Moore and Duncanson had traveled from Cincinnati to Johnson City, Tennessee, and then probably by stagecoach to Asheville on the rough road known as the Buncombe Turnpike.

May We All Remember Well: A Journal of the History and Cultures of Western North Carolina, Volume 1 was published in 1997 with a detail of the painting spread across the front and back covers. Andrew's study included a biography of Duncanson, a discussion of his other works, and speculation as to what might have happened if James Washington Patton, the largest owner of enslaved people in the region, and Duncanson, an African American, had met in 1850.

One day, Jerry called to say that I needed to go see Mary Parker; it was important, he said, and hinted that it concerned the painting. Jerry and I were in her dining room the next afternoon, under the watchful eyes of James Washington Patton and his wife, Henrietta, Mary's great-grandparents, whose portraits hung above the fireplace. In his essay, Andrew had suggested that Duncanson might have also painted the two portraits.

Mary's circumstances had changed, and she had been thinking about selling the painting "for a good little bit," but she couldn't abide the thought of it not hanging above the sideboard. She pointed a crooked finger at the painting. "I just enjoy looking at it," she said quietly.

We explored the idea of having a giclée print of the painting made and a frame to match the original. It could then be hung above the sideboard. Mary liked the idea. What an honor it would be for me to sell this important southern landscape of Western North Carolina.

In the following weeks, two prints were made. One was given to Mary and the other to the Colburn Mineral Museum in memory of her brother, Frank Parker. Mary was pleased with the print resting above the sideboard and indicated that the proceeds from the sale of the painting were also go to the Colburn Museum.

A few days later, we took Mary to our auction facility on Tunnel Road in Asheville so she could become familiar with our work and meet Laura, our painting specialist. We explained absentee and phone bidding and showed her where her painting would be exhibited. The galleries were overflowing that day, with 1,100 lots of furniture, paintings, silver, jewelry, porcelains, art glass, and architectural elements on display for the next auction. "I am fascinated by this. How do you keep it all straight?" she asked, shaking her head. I wondered too.

Several months later, on May 31, 2003, we sold *A View of Asheville* before a gallery crowded with interested people, including several museums and collectors. The painting was purchased by an agent on behalf of the Greenville County Museum of Art, Greenville, South Carolina. The painting sold for $325,000, the Asheville Art Museum active in the bidding until about $250,000.

Greenville, South Carolina, is about sixty miles south of Asheville and, like Asheville, was situated on the Buncombe Turnpike, the same turnpike that had delivered Robert Duncanson to Asheville in 1850. More than 150 years later, the painting traveled south about sixty miles to Greenville, on roads parallel to the route of the Buncombe Turnpike.

In the years that followed, until she died in 2012 at ninety-seven years of age, Mary Parker enjoyed the likeness of her painting above her sideboard, her family still looking out over the little village she loved so deeply.

....

When considering the history and importance of Duncanson's painting of Asheville, I confronted Asheville's, and my family's, history with enslaved people. In 1830, James Patton, ancestor of Mary Parker, had enslaved 50 people, the most in Buncombe County. By 1850, the year Duncanson painted *A View of Asheville*, 12.8 percent of the population of Buncombe County were enslaved: 1,717 people. By 1860, James Washington Patton had enslaved 68 people.

One of my great-great-grandfathers, Elijah Jennings, who lived in rural East Tennessee and fought as a Confederate soldier in the Civil War, had also enslaved people. In the 1850 Anderson County, Tennessee, "Schedule of Slave Inhabitants" (the year Duncanson painted *A View of Asheville*), three enslaved people are listed under "Elijah Jinnings [*sic*]":

one male 40 years old
one female 13 years old
one male 9 years old

Under the heading "Color," all three are listed as "Black."

What words would one choose to explain to a nine-year-old boy that he was owned by someone? Perhaps words were not necessary, as enslavement may have been made clear by the weight of custom and the fear of punishment. For years, the boy may have understood that he could be bought or sold like any other property, an animal or a sack of corn.

As I think of this nine-year-old boy who lived on a marginal farm near Clinton, Tennessee, I try to imagine his life as an enslaved child. How did the world look to him? What possibilities, if any, did he envision for himself? These questions help me understand more fully the impulse to take down Confederate monuments, in particular the seventy-five-foot stone obelisk in Asheville's Pack Square, known as the Vance Monument.

Zebulon Vance was born in 1830, twelve miles north of Asheville, to a family that had enslaved eighteen people. He fought in the Civil War, rose to the rank of colonel in the Confederate army, and was elected governor of North Carolina and a US senator. In all these positions, Vance was a steadfast defender of enslavement.

In a popular Vance lecture, "The Scattered Nation," he describes the "African negro [*sic*]" as descending from "barbarian tribes who for four thousand years have contributed nothing to . . . civilization."

Due in part to demands related to the murder of George Floyd, the Asheville City Council voted on March 23, 2021, by a vote of six to one, to have the Vance Monument removed. The last of the polished stone sections were taken down on May 30, 2021, and stored in an unidentified location.

If I were able, and permitted to, I would have helped lift the speckled granite blocks off the pedestal where they, for 124 years, had celebrated the life of Zebulon Vance.

LIGHT

In 2003, we purchased a former furniture store on Tunnel Road in Asheville and moved our business to that location. On a pleasant Saturday morning in our new facility, the preview for our auction had ended, and auction goers were gradually taking their seats. Some still lingered in the coffee and pastry area at the back of the gallery. The tape recorder had been turned on; I had finished my opening remarks and had read the terms of sale. It was the relaxed beginning of a two-day auction. Over 1,200 lots lay ahead of us.

A well-dressed woman scurried to her seat on the front row. She wore a colorful summer shirt and white linen slacks, accentuated by a large designer belt buckle. She threw a quick smile my way, perhaps a mild apology for her slight interruption, and I sent a friendly wave back. We encouraged our clients to make careful inspections of any items on which they planned to bid and suggested the use of a flashlight and a magnifying glass. I had seen the woman examining several pieces during the preview and was pleased to note that she had prepared carefully for her bidding. As the woman sat down, she put her magnifying glass and its leather case in her purse and pushed her cigar-shaped flashlight into the large front left pocket of her linen slacks. She studied the auction program and her notes.

Perhaps twenty minutes later, she bid on an old toleware watering can, the estimate $150–$250. As she shifted her body slightly to raise her bid card, the flashlight went on and created a bright signal about six inches below her belt buckle. Every time she bid, I saw the light.

I was close to laughing but looked away to distract myself. She bid two or three times on the watering can, the light faithfully sending forth its vivid signal with each bid. After the watering can sold to another bidder, I was able to slowly gather my composure.

Half an hour later, as she bid on a burlwood bowl, it happened again. As she raised her card, the light beamed its powerful beacon. In my strained efforts to maintain composure, my face became rearranged and frozen— prohibited laughter the most delicious. As she was sitting on the front row, it was impossible to ignore. As soon as the bowl sold, I turned off the microphone and pretended to be coughing, bent over and hiding her from my view, as even the sight of her triggered the possibility of uncontrollable laughter.

An hour later, a rustic painted chair came up. She raised her card, but the light just flickered, a signal, I assumed, that she was hesitant, unsure of her bid. I was grateful when she pulled her card down. At one point, she stood and walked to the back of the gallery, presumably for a cup of coffee. I wondered if anyone else had seen the light.

....

An hour later, she bid again, this time on a Cherokee basket. I could no longer look her way. Just the thought of the light threw me onto the threshold of more suppressed laughter. I was unable to inhale or exhale, tears pouring down my face and running down my nose, my body sprained from my efforts to not laugh. I couldn't go on.

I was about to ask Fulton to take over the auction for a while, he a Rock of Gibraltar in crisis settings. But just then, a woman on our staff knelt beside the woman and told her about her flashlight and explained that I had seen the light. At last, she turned it off and glanced my way with a second smile. I sent her a second friendly wave.

This little light of mine
I'm gonna let it shine
Let it shine, let it shine, let it shine

PAINT

Late in the summer of 2005, Fulton and Jerry returned from a house call, excited about a painted chest they had brought back with them. They carried it proudly and placed it front and center in of our gallery, an exhibit of one. It was a New Hampshire chest-on-chest, made in the late eighteenth or early nineteenth century by one of the cabinetmakers of the Dunlap school. It had the characteristic black mustache-shaped skirt below the drawers and typically small cabriole legs. But most remarkable was the surface: it retained its original paint, which had never been scraped or stripped, a rare and desirable feature.

I asked Jerry about the woman who had consigned the chest. He said she lived alone and was in financial trouble; she could not pay all her medical bills, especially her prescriptions that cost several thousand dollars a month. While Jerry and Fulton watched, she had opened the drawers of the chest and stacked her clothing on her bed, commenting that the chest was the last piece she owned of any value, although she didn't think it was worth very much. Our catalog description read as follows:

> Dunlap School high chest, maple and white pine, the upper case with molded cornice above five lipped and graduated drawers, the lower case fitted with two drawers, the upper being a faux-fronted double drawer, all with realistic faux grain paint and faux-painted inlay, and original brass bale-handles. New Hampshire, probably Major John Dunlap or Samuel Dunlap, 1780–1800, 80½ × 41 × 20½ in. Appears to retain its original brasses and grain-painted surface, shrinkage cracks

in case appear to post-date grain painting suggesting that the paint is original (see detail), bottom three drawers of upper case and bottom drawer of lower case fitted with later locks, minor losses, chips and cracks to painted surface, cracks due to shrinkage, other minor flaws, feet and knee returns appear to be intact (detailed photos available).

When we completed our evaluation of the chest, I called the owner and told her it would carry an estimate of $40,000–$80,000, with some potential beyond that. She seemed pleased but not as excited about this information as many clients would have been if they heard numbers such as these; it was almost as though she had not heard the amounts. She mentioned that she had lots of bills to pay and began listing her current expenses in detail, most related to chronic health problems.

A few days later, she called back and asked if we could give her an advance on the sale of the chest so she could make her mortgage payment and pay several other bills. We advanced her several thousand dollars against the sale of the chest.

Andrew, who at the time was head of American Furniture at Christie's New York, was back in Asheville a few weeks later and found an original inscription on the side of a lower drawer, indicating for whom the chest had been made. We were able to confirm through census records that the name was that of the chest's first owner, and most importantly, when we mentioned the name to the consignor, she said it was one of her ancestors. The chest had apparently never been out of her family, nor had it ever been offered for sale, very appealing credentials to potential buyers.

It was always intriguing when Andrew came home for a visit and examined what we were selling in the next auction. He had the uncanny ability to find significant details we could include in our descriptions. A few years later, he and his family moved back to Asheville, and he joined me in the business. From then on, the business grew and began setting records, the highest prices realized for several paintings, folk art, and important pieces of Southern furniture.

When we began advertising the chest, the response was immediate, several people flying in a few days later. It was not the most ornate Dunlap chest, but the surface and the provenance made it a very desirable example. When we offered it for auction, on September 24, 2005, it brought $276,000, including buyer's premium.

The night of the sale, I called the consignor to report the surprising news. After a long pause, she said she couldn't believe the chest was worth anything close to that number and asked several times if someone was really going to pay that for it. She had not attended the auction, so I mentioned that we had a recording of the day's proceedings and she was welcome to come in and listen to the tape, a clear recounting of the sale of her chest. She said she would come the next morning.

When she walked into our gallery she was wearing winter clothes and walked with the weight of heavy sadness, her face gray and drawn, without expression. She stood off to one side of the front counter, her head close to the tape recorder, her eyes closed, repeating that section of the tape over and over again, apparently trying to embrace this information. It seemed as though she wanted for this to have happened but was afraid to believe it. I wanted to help her not to be afraid, but I was not sure how to do this.

After she had listened to the tape, she stood and looked around our large auction area, her eyes skipping about but not landing on anything. She thanked me for selling the chest for her, but her thanks were subdued, almost obligatory, as though she still could not commit to the truthfulness of all that had happened. She may have thought that sometimes things that are too good to be true turn out not to be true.

She asked when she would be paid. I replied that the buyer had thirty days to pay for the chest, and as soon as he did, we would issue her check. She cleared her throat and steadied herself for what she was about to say. "I want to be paid in cash," she announced, her words clear and not in the form of a question. I guided her into my office so we could talk in private. She sat on the front half of her chair, more alert and focused now.

I had visions of an elderly woman walking around with a quarter of a million dollars in her purse, if it would even have fit in her purse. "I really don't think that would be a good idea," I answered.

"I don't see why you can't do that." She mentioned her unpaid bills again.

Maybe she wanted to see that pile of money on a table in front of her and feel its weight in her hands, to hold several thick packs of hundred-dollar bills with paper bands around them, each marked $10,000, twenty-five of these squared-up piles arranged in neat rows in front of her. Perhaps the scent of new ink would be in the air. This tangible, undeniable moment would be more trustworthy than a piece of paper with a number written on it. Maybe she feared that this money would disappear as suddenly as it had appeared in her life. Maybe she wanted to keep it within her sight. Hold it. Grip it with her fingers.

Perhaps belief in anything was an impossible luxury for her, even this windfall. Maybe her days were filled with painful physical and emotional dilemmas, exhaustion, loneliness. And no matter how needed and welcome this money might be, it was also a disruption requiring time and energy, an added weight to her burdens. Many decisions would need to be made, decisions she may not have been equipped to make, mired as she was in the details of her current situation. Perhaps she understood that many of her problems could not be solved with money. I looked at her anxious face, her stooped shoulders, her watery eyes, and wondered if she no longer had any capacity to even imagine changes in her life.

"I understand the temptation to hold this money in your hands," I said, "but I really don't want to do that. There are too many risks." I suggested that when we received the check, we would call her. Then Fulton, our security man, would go with her to her bank and stand with her until the check was safely deposited. After a lengthy discussion, and much to my relief, she finally agreed to this plan. Two weeks later, the check arrived, and Fulton escorted her to the bank without incident.

In several cases when a client of ours had received a large check, family members would tell us a year or two later that the money had been wasted, bad decisions made, leaving the client no better off financially or emotionally. I hoped that this would not be the case with this woman, but I feared for her. She seemed trapped by her unpaid bills but had not mentioned using the money to solve her financial problems.

The chest, however, soared to a new home. Slightly over two years later, in January 2008, the chest reappeared in an online article published by *incollect*. The great New Hampshire chest-on-chest with original surface was now in the collection of Jerry and Susan Lauren, he the brother of Ralph Lauren and the executive vice president of men's design at Polo Ralph Lauren. The Laurens had assembled an exceptional collection of American folk art, which was displayed in their gallery-like apartment in Manhattan. The article included photos of their collection, including one of the chest we had sold. Jerry Lauren described it as follows: "It is perfectly grained with an almost 3-D effect. To me this is true folk art. The wood was not valuable so they did their best to simulate fine furniture by using paint. It's all original and pristine. There is such wonderful negative space beneath the chest, and Susan has always enjoyed the shape of the Queen Anne legs. When we placed it against the wall, it was like, 'Wow!' The wall was waiting for it. It's a masterpiece."

SILVER

On a busy spring day in 2002, Mr. Williams, who looked to be in his seventies, carried a mahogany case with brass handles into our auction house. He positioned it on a table in our consignment area and stared at it for a moment, as though he might be listening to it. As I introduced myself, I offered to help him unpack, but he declined with a slight wave of his hand. The leather elbow pads on his gray sweater were burnished from wear. His deliberate movements suggested a cautious man, but he was otherwise unremarkable in his appearance and bearing. Over the next decade, my interactions with him would remind me that the most unassuming individuals often have the most to teach us about ourselves.

He slowly untied several blue flannel storage rolls and laid out a set of sterling silver flatware, a complete service for twelve plus serving pieces. He carefully arranged the set in neat stacks and then beside each placed a card with hand-printed notes, "12 luncheon forks, 7½ inches."

I was pleased to see a large set of Audubon, one of the most sought-after Tiffany sterling silver flatware patterns, named in honor of John James Audubon, the well-known nineteenth- century American ornithologist and artist. Mr. Williams looked up at me and said the set had been in his family for several generations. "I'm interested in selling this silver, if it brings enough money," he said softly. It was too early in our conversation to ask what he meant by "enough money."

Tiffany had introduced this pattern in 1871, during an era of the decorative arts known as the Aesthetic Movement. This style celebrated the distinguishing motifs of exotic cultures, including Moorish, Egyptian, Arabesque, and, in the case of this silver, the Japanese taste. Eight species of exquisite birds perched and hovered among arrays of elegant flowers on the handles of the silverware in scenes derived from Japanese paintings, the fine details of each piece raised in meticulous, low relief silver.

Someone in Mr. Williams's family had been attracted to this flatware pattern, possibly for a wedding or silver anniversary gift. Perhaps someone in his family was drawn to the *idea* of owning a set of this famous silver, more attracted to ownership than to the silent birds and demure, finely rendered flowers. The silver could lie modestly on a formally furnished dining table, flanking the Flora Danica plates and the Saint Louis crystal stemware, waiting for a guest to ask the host or hostess about the unusual silverware. Then the owner could graciously describe Audubon's birds and flowers and the fame of this pattern. Perhaps just considering the idea of ownership had been a sufficient pleasure for someone.

I told Mr. Williams that his flatware would attract considerable interest and that we would be pleased to offer it in an upcoming auction. I could imagine significant competition for his set of flatware, but I understated my enthusiasm, as I didn't want to unnerve him with excessive praise. Several weeks earlier, I had been extravagant in my admiration of a fine painting, only to have the client say, "Well, if it's that great, I think I'll just hold on to it for a while."

I described the consignment process, referring to our consignment agreement, a contract he would need to sign if he decided to sell his silver. We would write a careful description of the flatware, create a high and low estimate for the set, and then photograph the silver for our catalog, website, and other advertising venues.

As I worked my way through the terms of the contract, he listened without comment, occasionally turning over a fork or spoon, perhaps enjoying the familiarity of each piece. When I read the clause that stated, "Neither the consignor nor his agent may bid on the consigned property," he held up his hand to stop me. "If they don't bring enough, I'm going to bid on them," he said without looking up.

I explained that we announced at our auctions that owners and their friends and relatives were prohibited from bidding, artificially raising the selling price. Some people don't trust auctioneers, I continued, and worry that auctioneers take bids "off the wall" or have shills planted in the audience from whom they would take fictitious bids. I told him as decisively as I could that this business rested on trust. I had been witness to several auctioneers artificially boosting bids and had seen how this could erode confidence in an auctioneer's reputation. Clever auctioneers, working rapidly, can invent bids very easily.

Mr. Williams could not know this intersection: my desire to create an unerringly honest auction and my equally compelling aspirations to offer outstanding examples of the decorative arts. He listened to my homily on ethics without comment. Finally, he said again, "I'm not going to sell the silver unless I can bid on it."

I repeated that I thought it would do very well at auction but that he could not bid on the silver and that this was "not negotiable." I congratulated myself a bit for enforcing our policy.

As neither of us seemed inclined to bridge the impasse between us, he slowly repacked the silver into the mahogany case. We shook hands, and he left.

About six months later, Mr. Williams called again. "I've been thinking about selling the silver flatware I brought in, and I want to discuss it some more," he said evenly. I was delighted, but I had not forgotten his plans to bid on his silver.

We greeted each other briefly as he lowered the mahogany case onto the same table in the consignment area. Then, without comment, he spent a few minutes walking through the gallery with a catalog I had given him, stopping to look at the ornate French furniture and old Persian carpets offered in the upcoming sale. I was encouraged by his interest in what we were selling. Maybe he had made peace with the prospect of selling his silver at auction.

As we sat to discuss his silver, he did not unpack the flatware and the carefully written notes as he had before; instead, he asked how the auctions were conducted. Where did I begin the bidding? What if the bidding stopped at a low price? What happened if no one bid on a particular lot?

I answered all his queries carefully and explained that we turn down a large percentage of the property we see and choose only those objects for which we have a strong market. I asked what value he put on his set of Audubon flatware; at what selling price would he be comfortable? I showed him catalogs and prices realized for other Tiffany silver flatware we had offered in the past year. He did not reply, still holding with both hands the auction catalog I had given him and glancing briefly at the mahogany case.

He looked at me, his face without expression, and said only, "I need to be able to bid on the silver if it is going too low." He spoke in a pleasant manner, but I still felt the firmness of his decision.

"I'm sorry, we just can't do that." We seemed to be having the same conversation over and over again, but I couldn't find any way to keep the discussion alive. As before, we shook hands, and he left with no further comments.

I wondered about Mr. Williams's attachment to his silver. Perhaps his need to bid on the Tiffany flatware was not related to money but to his need to be an active participant in the final disposition of a family treasure, to in some way control the outcome. Perhaps the Audubon silver service carried an irrevocable grid of family history or deeply felt memories of a family member, and he could not picture his family no longer owning the beautiful silver flatware. Had some fixed marker in his life shifted or been uprooted? Or, if the silver left the sanctuary of his family, perhaps it would trigger a hidden, more complex fear, one he could not name. Perhaps there was no price with which he would be comfortable.

Several years later, Mr. Williams called again, reintroduced himself, and said he needed to begin "downsizing" and had decided to sell the set of Tiffany Audubon and other silver flatware. I remembered him and our past discussions quite clearly. When he returned to our office, after a few friendly exchanges, he unpacked his silver and again arranged the flatware in orderly stacks. I went over our contract and the process of consignment, much as I had before.

"We must be very clear that you will not bid on your silver," I said slowly, watching his face for reactions. There were none, and I saw no sign that he was prepared to let go of the silver until he reached for his pen and signed the consignment agreement. I repeated my concerns, saying that if he bid on any of his lots of silver, I would have to stop the auction and withdraw that lot. I was hoping for a reaction other than his stoic demeanor, something to signal agreement, but he stood up slowly and left without a word or gesture.

We advertised the silver extensively, highlighting it in our color brochures mailed to several thousand buyers in fifty states. It was mentioned conspicuously in our ads in the *Newtown Bee* and the *Maine Antique Digest*. Collectors contacted us, asking for photos and a detailed listing of the Tiffany flatware. Several made reservations to bid on the silver by phone.

Several days before the auction, I called Mr. Williams to ask if he had seen the photo of his silver in the brochure and to see if he was planning on attending the auction. He replied that he had received his brochure and was indeed coming to the auction. I asked if he understood our terms of sale. He said, "I'm OK," but I was not reassured.

He arrived before the auction began and sat several rows back from the podium. He held the auction catalog in his hands and seemed to be reading the descriptions of the lots, only occasionally glancing up or making a note with his pen. There were many lots of silver flatware in the auction, and some Tiffany silver had been consigned by other owners.

When his first lot came up for sale, I was poised and ready, and sure enough, he raised his hand to bid. My suspicions had been confirmed. I announced, "Sir, we have discussed this at length. You may not bid on your own property at this auction, and this lot is withdrawn." He made no response, and his posture did not change.

I had anticipated this moment, and for an instant, I felt the rightness of what I had done; he had bid on his silver, and I had done what I said I would do. I had defended my ground.

But real, unmistakable awkwardness hung in the air. There seemed to be no symmetry in what had happened. Several of my staff stared at me, puzzled, though they were fully aware of our history with Mr. Williams. A few minutes later, one came to the podium. I turned off the microphone and heard her say, "He was not bidding on his silver. The lot he bid on belonged to someone else."

I had assumed he was only a seller, never considering that he might also be a buyer. I had been blinded by my preoccupation with his possible violation of our policy, my need to protect the honesty of our work. I had set the stage for this to happen and had found what I was looking for.

He was a shy man on unfamiliar ground, not out to challenge my rules, and he had not violated my request not to bid on his property. I had humiliated Mr. Williams in public, and he left the auction soon after this happened. I struggled through the remainder of the auction, unable to alter what I had done. I tried calling him that evening and several times over the next few days, but no one answered. I wrote a heartfelt letter of the deepest apology I could fashion but received no response to ease my despair.

I never saw Mr. Williams again, but his silver did reappear.

To my surprise, he came by our facility a few months later and consigned all his silver, including the Tiffany Audubon flatware. I was out of town when he made his appointment with Robin. She told me later that neither he nor she had mentioned the prior events. We sold his silver several weeks later, and it did very well, higher than the high estimates, though he did not attend the auction.

About six years later, I saw Mr. Williams's obituary in the paper, my recollection of him and his Audubon silver lodged permanently in my memory. Since the incident, I had come to admire his restraint in not seeking reprisal or escalating the conflict. He apparently had no investment in defending his public persona. He never expressed any anger or recrimination to me or anyone else on our staff. He made no complaint and in no way sought retribution, traits I respected.

How sad, I reflected, that I knew so little about this man. I had looked at him in only one way and had found in him only one trait, a perceived failing. Maybe we could have had a conversation about John James Audubon and his creation of over 400 illustrations of American birds and his documentation of 21 new species. I could have turned over a piece of Mr. Williams's silver and asked whose monogram it bore and how the silver came into his family.

Several months later, on a warm July afternoon in 2011, Mr. Williams's widow came to see me, bearing two outstanding pieces of Pisgah Forest pottery to consign. She was moving to Chicago and didn't want to take the large vases with her. She wore bright summer clothes and a stylish straw hat. When she spoke, she held her hands together in a slightly celebratory gesture, as if she might have been singing.

I wanted to say something about the Tiffany silver incident but had trouble finding the first words. Finally, I said, "That was a difficult moment several years ago with the silver."

She looked at me kindly and said without hesitation, "Oh, don't worry. You both did OK with the whole thing." Her words glided lightly through the air, like the flight of silent, exquisite birds.

LEDGER

At an appraisal event near Hickory, North Carolina, I was one of three appraisers working for a winter afternoon in 2008 to support a small local museum. The appraisals were part of a membership promotion; if you became a new member at the level of "patron," the highest and most expensive level of membership, one of the perks was a free appraisal of one object. The event was staged in a large social room; a long, noisy line spread out the door and down an adjoining hall.

Midafternoon, a woman approached my table with light, fluid steps, almost as though she was slightly afloat, and held out a book as though delivering a gift. She laid the worn, thick volume on the table, the front of the book facing me. She held out a hand, saying, "My name is Agatha, and I brought a book for you to look at." The red fore-edges and half-leather binding suggested it might be a ledger.

As we shook hands, I apologized for her long wait. I guessed she was in her forties, several strands of white visible in her hair. She wore hiking clothes and old, very worn boots. She smiled warmly as she spoke, as though we already knew each other.

"I found this book in an old house I bought several years ago. It was on a high shelf in a closet of an unused upstairs bedroom with a few books on Tennessee history," she told me. "But I don't know if it came from Tennessee or not."

I had listened to many owners' stories about their possessions; they ranged from the credible, to the suspect, to finely crafted fiction. I had learned to be cautious in trusting all I heard, as once a man had brought in stolen property. And though this woman's story seemed rather loose, easy to make up, and hard to verify, her kind and gentle manner weighed in on the side of believable.

She sat down and folded her hands as I opened the impressive book, a ledger recording transactions at a grain mill from 1850 to 1862. The inside cover was marked "Book II." Each entry noted the date, name of the customer, type and quantity of grain brought in, the yield, and how payment was made—cash or in kind. Several entries listed long-standing, unpaid debts. The entire document was carefully written, potentially an important primary source for a scholar, though it lacked the name of the mill or its owner or its location, which might have been recorded in "Book I." Agatha watched me silently as I gently turned several pages.

I was delighted. I would enjoy exploring this document with this woman named Agatha, as I have always been attracted to mills—not just to the rushing water, the great vertical waterwheels powering the impossibly heavy millstones, but also to the creation of energy based solely on the curated use of water and gravity. And I often imagined people sitting around a mill, gossiping, telling stories while they waited for their flour to be ready.

Despite the long line of people waiting for an appraisal, I was in no hurry to finish this discussion. I told Agatha that in 1997, I had assisted in a survey of water-powered mills along Reems Creek, a small river near where I lived in Western North Carolina. Most of the structures were gone, but several elderly residents remembered the location and history of the mills and the commerce and social networks they engendered. A few had old photos of the mills, and two families had used old millstones as decorations in their yard.

I told Agatha that I especially enjoyed learning the local vocabulary for mill-related words: a turn of corn, race, burr mill, stone dresser, flume. Many people spoke of the sounds of grain being ground, the wooden buildings shaking a bit, vibrating. One woman said an old mill she often frequented as a child had "trembled" when it was grinding corn.

I ended my ruminations and shifted back to Agatha and the large book in front of us. Assuming she wanted to know its value, I pointed out that some objects have great historic or archival value but not necessarily high monetary value. If her ledger was specific to a place or to a person or family, it could be of great interest to an archive or repository of documents for a specific region, particularly because it included several years of the Civil War.

She responded quickly, smiling again and saying that she would never sell the ledger and was not interested in money. "I am here because I wanted to show you the ledger, and I am hoping you can help me figure out who wrote it. I'm a baker and I would like to know who these people were." Her eyes danced a bit.

I told her it would be very difficult to find out who owned the mill and its location. I suggested she might be able to track something down in census records for the state of Tennessee, the only available clue. Pick several men's last names from the ledger, I began, very unusual names, unlikely to show up more than once, and look for them in the 1850 or 1860 census. Or take an oft-repeated last name in the ledger and see if any clusters of that name appear in a particular county. I said some census records list occupations and that she might look for millers or mill workers. I added that county historical societies and regional archives might be helpful. "You will be very lucky to find the answer to your question, but this is at least a way to begin."

As I spoke, I noticed that Agatha didn't bother to write down any of my suggestions. Instead, when I finished, she began a story. "I was adopted," she told me. "I don't know anything about my real family's history, but I am drawn to this ledger and feel close to this time and this way of life; people took their wheat to the mill, it was ground by the miller, and they went home with bags of flour and baked their bread." Though her hands appeared to be strong from her work as a baker, she gestured with delicate, articulate movements as she spoke. I imagined her hands kneading dough and pulling freshly baked loaves out of an oven with a wooden peel. She said she liked the idea of our bread coming from the earth and the simple, unencumbered transactions with a miller. She added that sometimes she sat holding the ledger, wondering if she was a descendant of whoever wrote the document, if perhaps she was part of the family who had owned and run the mill.

Agatha looked at me earnestly, one hand pointing at two open pages of the ledger. "Mr. Brunk, do you think this is a woman's handwriting? I know in my heart that this was written by a woman." I moved to the end of the table, and she scooted her chair to the end so we could both look at the book. We began turning the pages together, she carefully raising the top corner of a page and I, often with both hands, turning the fragile, slightly stiff pages. With a magnifying glass we examined the block-like letters, written in thin lines of blue ink, with occasional tiny serifs at the corners. Some letters and numbers had swirls at the end that circled back over the entry; the y's had long downward loops, and the capital letters were almost always decorated with partial coils or springs. She pointed to several spaces between lines and near the end of several pages that had been decorated with flourishes: finely rendered, feather-like crosshatches and tiny sketches, mostly of boxes. One might have been an angel. I imagined an older person, laboring for many hours, repeatedly dipping his or her pen in a bottle of ink, frequently pressing the tip of the pen against a blotter. The writer had created an improvised, personal font of sorts.

As the afternoon progressed, the level of noise and commotion in the social room increased, but Agatha and I were deeply absorbed in the iconography of the ledger and no longer noticed the distractions of people waiting in line to have their treasures evaluated.

I said the ledger had been written with remarkable skill, probably by one person, but I couldn't tell if it was the work of a woman. Whoever had done this, I added, had created a genuine work of art, a vernacular treasure. I said the writing seemed to create a rhythm, not unlike a line of music, all the improvisation related to a theme. Agatha beamed and clapped her hands.

I asked if she had ever seen or been in a grain mill. She stared at the ledger, preoccupied with the fine script, and offered no answer.

I wondered out loud how she came to be a baker. She folded her hands again and said she had been teaching fourth grade in a local elementary school for several years when she was asked by a friend of her adoptive parents if she would be interested in a part-time job, working from 3:00 to 7:00 a.m. in a small bakery before she began her day as a teacher. She accepted the offer and knew immediately that this job was meant for her. After finishing the school year several months later, she accepted a full-time job at the bakery. Her work involved baking all the bread but not the cakes and pastries, which again suited her perfectly.

She itemized the characteristics of the many flours she had learned to use in her new job: whole and white wheat, barley, buckwheat, rye, and oat flours. She explained in detail the chemistry of using yeast to leaven bread and said she loved the fact that it was a simple microorganism, a common fungus, that created the magic of rising bread.

She talked excitedly about the various shapes into which bread could be created: loaves, buns, rounds, hearts, crosses, baguettes. As she described kneading dough and forming a loaf, she often pushed her hands together and then pulled her agile fingers apart, back and forth, as though she was playing a small concertina.

I was attracted to this woman and her passion for making bread. I imagined wearing a white apron, carrying bags of flour, helping her make dough, my hair dusted white. I had never done any of those things. What a pleasant surprise to meet a woman so committed to her work and so articulate about the essential elements of baking bread.

Abruptly, she asked if I knew anything about Saint Agatha, the patron saint of bakers. I said I did not. She told me that several years earlier she'd looked into the meaning of her name and found that Saint Agatha of Sicily had lived AD 231–251 and that her life of faith and devotion is celebrated every year in Catania, Sicily, during the first week of February. As a patron saint, she offers blessings and protection to bakers and others who support their work, including millers.

Not sure how to respond, I turned the conversation away from sainthood and mentioned a gristmill I had seen in 2008 on the remote island of Unst, the northernmost of the Shetland Islands, off the northeast coast of Scotland. I said I'd been reminded of this place when she talked about a simple lifestyle, walking to a nearby mill to have grain turned into flour, baking bread with the flour. "Oh, yes," she said, nodding her head vigorously, "please tell me everything about the mill."

For several nights, during the first week of February, I had stayed in a bed and breakfast near Haroldswick and met the owners, Irene and Tony Mouat. I soon became intrigued by their efforts to restore a small hillside mill, said to have been used in some form for several hundred years and which had served the needs of perhaps two or three extended families. Tony and Irene were excited, as the next morning they were planning to test for the first time the results of many months of work. They would not be grinding any wheat but checking the movement of water and the mechanics of the mill. They invited me to join them.

Early the next morning, cloudy and windy, we walked the short distance to a small, unremarkable hill, the pastures in shades of brown and gray, Tony carrying a shovel and hammer. The wind pushed against us without pause and carried the grip of cold.

We walked partway up the hill to a small body of water. Centuries of erosion from the runoff of a spring farther up the slope had created a grassy pit, which Tony had boarded up to create a small, deep pool, the mill pond. He had constructed a wooden trough, a sluice, over a hundred feet long to carry the water down to the mill, and a gate, which would be opened to start the mill.

On several other occasions I had traveled in the Shetland Islands and the Outer Hebrides and had seen several of these grain mills, often called Norse mills—simple, water-powered devices with horizontal waterwheels.

They operated without gears, the shaft of the waterwheel also the shaft of the millstones mounted above.

Agatha nodded often as I spoke, apparently savoring every detail, as though she was familiar with the workings of a mill. Her hands were folded again, resting on the ledger.

When we arrived at the mill, I saw a long-standing stone structure, roughly ten by twenty feet, about five feet of which was visible above ground and six feet below the grassy sod. The stone walls had been dry stacked, with no visible mortar, as were the many miles of walls bordering fields in this region. On the corners of the partially collapsed top of Tony and Irene's mill, I saw fragments of the original sod roof, common to these buildings.

The sluice entered the mill just below ground level. Tony had built the waterwheel, a vertical beam with five large red-painted wooden blades, canted for maximum effectiveness, which stood next to the end of the sluice in the small, cave-like underground space. Two millstones rested on top of each other on the wet floor. The stationary bed stone sat under the runner stone, which would circulate to create grist, the coarse first run to create fine flour.

Irene positioned herself at the sluice gate, and Tony, inside the mill, after making some adjustments, gave her the signal to open the gate. Water poured down the sluice and into the mill, and soon the waterwheel rotated in proper style. Tony let out a whoop of victory as Irene came running down the hill. They stood in the muddy water, staring at the waterwheel, its blades heaving and sloshing. Irene said all they needed now was to build a new roof and mount the millstones above the waterwheel.

I wondered if Agatha pictured herself climbing a hill like this with a bucket of dry wheat and slowly pouring it into the hopper above the millstones, repeating the ancient rituals of families in this region. I tried to explain to her how this experience in Unst had affected me. The basic design of this simple device was similar to a multitude of comparable water mills, used for millennia in many cultures: water and grain from the earth to create food. How humble and unpretentious was Irene and Tony's labor to restore the ruin of the old mill, to make possible the revival of a universal, life-giving tradition. I was moved by their efforts and told Agatha that I remember clearly the sound of splashing water, the repeating thump of the waterwheel, Tony's shout of excitement.

Agatha became silent, staring at me with a look of wonder mixed with a curious sort of joy, neither of which I understood at that moment. She asked if the date, early February, when I visited Tony and Irene, was correct. I said yes.

Agatha, her eyes now closed, her face almost glowing, whispered. "Saint Agatha was there. The first week in February is the time of the festivals celebrating her life of faith and devotion. She was there, celebrating with Tony and Irene, and you, repairing the ruin of an old mill, which would now provide flour to bakers."

I had understood the experience differently than she, but I felt no urge to question her. It had been a unique, deeply personal moment for me. I felt connected to a specific, tangible cultural trait, a ritual, common in all its variations, to centuries of human experience.

We sat silently for a few moments, slowly shifting from the island of Unst back to the noisy social room.

Agatha described the moment when she first picked up the ledger. She had seen it many times, part of the closet clutter, but had never pulled it off the shelf. "I was standing on a ladder and needed both hands to pick it up. When I first held the book, a wave of current went through me. I had flashes of very old buildings, churches, rivers, crowds of people, none I had ever seen before. I didn't know what was happening." She said she had then fallen into a chair and hugged the book for several hours, tears in her eyes.

As Agatha ended her story, she opened a folder she had laid on the table and handed me a sheet of paper about half the size of a page of the ledger, written in exactly the same style: block letters, fine blue ink, delicate serifs, imaginative flourishes. The vertical lines creating spaces for entries matched the lines of the ledger. I asked if it was a loose page from the book before us. "I made this copy of part of page 36," she replied.

The word "forgery" jumped in front of me. I wondered if she had found an old blank ledger and filled it with invented content and stylized writing.

She became silent for a moment, staring at the open book, her face still spirited but more thoughtful. "Mr. Brunk, I need to explain something to you. I took a big chance when I brought this ledger to you, and I wasn't sure I would be able to tell you what I am about to say, but as we talked, I began to believe I could trust you." She looked at me with great kindness, as though searching for language, a foothold for what she was about to say.

She reached out to hold one of my hands and with shining eyes said in a clear voice, "For many years I wondered if I was Saint Agatha. I copied this page to test the idea that I might be her. I am a baker and have no artistic or writing skills." She said that as she copied this page of the ledger, her hand had moved across the page as though it was guided.

"Mr. Brunk, it all fit. By some miracle, my hand wrote this ledger, and now I am the guardian of this document.

"I am Saint Agatha.

"You see, Mr. Brunk, I was there with you in 1997, on Reems Creek, watching over the survey of old mills. I was there with you years later on the island of Unst watching Tony and Irene, blessing their work, sharing their joy in restoring an old mill. I am anywhere where the work of bakers and millers is celebrated or needs protection. I was in Ohio from 1850 to 1862, documenting the work of the Yoder family as I wrote this ledger. They were Mennonites who owned a large mill and served many families in central Ohio."

It was now clear to me that the ledger was not a forgery.

I asked why she'd brought the book in today. "I take it any place where I can call attention to the importance of the work of bakers and millers. I want people to be acquainted with the grain, the water, both from the earth, and the making of bread, which has been done for thousands of years." She added softly, "Bread is also used as a sacrament in the Christian church, 'the bread of life.'

"I was hoping we would have this conversation, and that you would be able to listen." Her voice was calm, grateful.

I claim no expertise in matters of the spirit and struggled to understand all that had happened in the last fifteen minutes. Had I been visited by a benevolent saint capable of moving through time and space, or had I met a baker with a remarkably fertile imagination? In any case, I was drawn to this woman and her work: a kind and nurturing presence seemingly incapable of malice in any form, looking for times and places in which she could offer support and blessings in service to what she believed carried elements of the sacred, a gentle being in a violent world.

She stood, the ledger in her arms, and turned quickly to leave. She took several steps and mouthed a silent "Thank you" as the next participant came to the table and began unpacking a porcelain bowl.

VASE

The most remarkable example of an unassuming object doing well in one of our auctions—unimaginably well—was a Chinese vase we sold in May 2009. The consignor had brought in a group of household furnishings she wanted to sell, saying she had financial troubles, and asked us to include anything we could in an upcoming auction. The yellow porcelain vase is the only piece I remember from the items she unpacked and arranged on a table in our consignment area. We agreed to sell the vase, and to help her a bit we took a few other pieces.

Ruby, our Asian specialist, cataloged the porcelain vase for our upcoming auction.

> Lot 800. Chinese *famille rose* vase, pear shape, flowers on yellow ground, sgraffito plumes, base and interior with turquoise enamel, base with red four-character seal mark for *Qianlong* period (1736–1795), 20th century, 12 in. Minor wear to gilt on rims. Estimate $400–$800.

After we advertised the vase with a photo in our color catalog, a steady procession of dealers and collectors came to examine it. They took photographs from many angles and used black lights and magnifying glasses to examine the surface in detail. No one found any damage or repairs. They held it in their hands and arms to understand its heft and balance. Most worked with it for an hour or more and approached the yellow vase gently, with an air of respect. We realized that for these people, there was something special about the vase.

Opinions about its age were mixed. Roughly half the people who examined it said they agreed with our description: it was a later copy. Others made no comment.

The vase came up for auction on a quiet Sunday afternoon, the second day of a two-day auction. Several people had left absentee bids, three staff members stood with phone bidders, and a scattering of people in the gallery entered the bidding immediately, including a woman standing in the back of the gallery with a cell phone pressed to her cheek. The bidding advanced very quickly and, in a few moments, had risen to $10,000, then $20,000, then $30,000. At $50,000, several floor bidders, one phone bidder, and the absentee bidders were finished. We had sold a gilt bronze Buddha a few years earlier for $65,000, and this piece seemed destined to reach that mark.

At $100,000, the young man showing the vase in the front of the gallery walked to a table and very carefully relaxed his grip as he positioned the vase in the center of a table.

There were two bidders left, a phone bidder in Australia and the lady with the cell phone in the back of the gallery. I jumped to $10,000 intervals, 120, 130, 140, 150, $160,000. At $500,000, I was having trouble breathing. Andrew picked up the vase and put it in the safe. I jumped to $25,000 intervals, 525, 550, 575, $600,000. The room was very quiet. Our entire staff of twenty-five stopped moving, frozen in wonder.

When the bidding reached $1 million, I paused. I was on unfamiliar ground and unsure of the next interval. The tension in the room eased when I asked, to a round of laughter, "Well, what's the next number?" The next number turned out to be the selling price: $1,245,000, including buyer's premium. The woman with the cell phone bought the vase, and when she returned the next day to make payment arrangements and pick up her purchase, she brought with her a fitted crate, made specifically for her Imperial vase.

When the auction was over, we called the consignor to share the remarkable news. She was stunned and spoke in broken sentences for a few moments. Then she asked several questions, mostly trying to determine if we were really having a conversation or if she was just imagining this moment.

About a week after the auction, the buyer called, asking if we could provide any history for the vase: Where had it come from? We in turn called the happy consignor and asked what she could tell us about the vase. She said she really didn't know much about it. She had bought it at a yard sale in Florida several years earlier. It had been a lamp; she had removed the brass mounts and kept the vase. The base had not been drilled to accommodate an electrical cord.

Slightly over five years later, on October 8, 2014, at a Sotheby's auction in Hong Kong titled "Fine Chinese Ceramics and Works of Art," the vase reappeared, as lot 3639. Its description did not suggest humility: "A Magnificent, Fine, and Extremely Rare, Yellow-Ground 'Yangcai' vase, Seal Mark and Period of *Qianlong*."

Yangcai translates roughly as "flowers on brocade," "*Qianlong*" the name of the reigning emperor.

In the Sotheby's catalog, the provenance for lot 3639 included the sale of the vase at Brunk Auctions in 2009.

Following are excerpts from the extensive descriptions and research notes included in the Sotheby's catalog:

> In form and decoration, this vase is amongst the most imaginative styles produced in the imperial kilns at *Jingdezhen.* . . . Its execution and design is [*sic*] particularly successful, . . . in the technique of sgraffito, where a formal design is incised into a solid pigment on leaves and flower petals.
>
> [The] intricately enameled . . . flower heads [include] stylized lotus, passiflora, anemone, lily, pomegranate, honeysuckle, iris, narcissus, rose, aster, peach blossom, and morning glory.
>
> *Yangcai* painted pieces were amongst the most prized types of porcelain in the *Qing* court, as well as being the type most treasured and admired by the emperor himself. Their special position in his collection is demonstrated by how he had them placed in his largest private quarters, the *Qianqinggong* ("Palace of Heavenly Purity"), located in the inner court of the Forbidden City.
>
> The porcelain inventory of the *Qing* imperial court archives, dated to the eighth day of the second month of the sixteenth year of *Qianlong*'s reign (corresponding to 1751), registers the delivery of a pair of "*yangcai*" vases . . . the only mention of pear-shaped *yangcai* vases in Court inventory.
>
> That it has been possible to find its original entry in the *Qing* imperial court archives makes it a truly magnificent legacy of the *Qianlong* reign.

The vase sold for $57,240,000 Hong Kong dollars, equivalent to $7,379,953 US dollars.

In the context of the highest prices paid for Chinese ceramics sold by Sotheby's in 2014, our vase ranked as the fourth most expensive, exceeded only by a Chicken Cup at $36.5 million, a Basin at $18.8 million, and a Dragon Jar at $12 million. In the rarefied and speculative climate in which important Chinese ceramics are bought and sold, the yellow *yangcai* vase may have changed hands several times since the Sotheby's auction. And the stakes would quickly escalate if the matching vase, the other half of the original pair, shows up in another yard sale.

The vase seems naked outside the highly valued place of honor it commanded in the emperor's collection of ceramics, as though part of its subtle beauty and radiance arose from the esteem with which it was held. As I look at color photos of the vase, I wonder who identified the twelve stylized flowers depicted on the sides. Was that knowledge offered by the maker of the vase, or were the names of those twelve species determined later by someone with a discerning eye and detailed knowledge of the flowers' structures, the contours and colors of the petals, stems, vines, and leaves? Humble morning glories and honeysuckle perhaps enjoying their finest hours. I was pleased that Ruby, who had cataloged the vase for our auction in 2009, had described the vase accurately: the pear shape, flowers on a yellow ground, sgraffito and enameled decoration, the seal marks and dates.

The money paid for the vase reflects an appreciation of its uniqueness, but it is also an exhibit of wealth and desire which might be a distraction. Seven million dollars might command more attention than the vase itself and could easily alter our vision when we look at it.

SNOW

I spent the first years of my life in Chicago, Illinois. Our family of four lived close to Midway Airport, where my father worked as a meteorologist. When I was eight years old, we moved to Lombard, a western suburb. There I began my first efforts to create a business: I mowed lawns, raked leaves, and worked in the gardens of our neighbors, and took some pride in the money I earned. When I was about twelve I created a "snow route" to shovel the sidewalks and driveways of a growing list of neighbors. I arranged verbal contracts with my clients whereby on any morning when an inch or more of snow had fallen, I would shovel their snow before I went to school at eight o'clock. I got up, usually around 3:30 a.m., and then returned after school to collect the money I had earned, typically about fifteen dollars. I enjoyed the money in my pocket but was equally attracted to the hard work involved. I seemed to thrive on it, especially when the snow was deep.

I loved those mornings tromping through the snow in my boots, stopping often to enjoy how quiet the neighborhood had become with a blanket of new snow. I loved snow and everything about it; I thought it was a gift from the heavens.

Later, as an adult living in the Asheville area, my affection for snow only increased. I usually owned a four-wheel drive vehicle and had no fear of driving on ice and snow. I would drive around in snowstorms, admiring the piles and drifts.

Whenever we had an auction scheduled during winter months, I would watch the weather forecasts carefully but always downplay any threat of snow and its consequences as being exaggerated. Clients from South Carolina and

Georgia would call to ask how much snow we had when the closest snow was in Arkansas or Illinois. I always told worried clients we would not cancel an auction unless we lost power and telephone service and I couldn't get to the auction myself, which was very unlikely since our house was only two miles from our auction gallery and I would walk there if necessary.

Early one January in 2004, we held a two-day auction at the Haywood Park Trade Mart in downtown Asheville. January auctions were often our largest of the year, and this was no exception: two full days of American and European furniture and accessories, silver, pottery, jewelry, paintings, carpets, a grand piano, country furniture.

The forecast for late Sunday, day two of the auction, mentioned the possibility of light snow. I reassured many anxious people that we would be finished Sunday afternoon and that the forecast of snow didn't always mean it would snow. This time I was wrong.

Sleet and light snow began as the temperature began falling early Saturday afternoon. The snow began so suddenly that many people who had planned to bolt for home with the first few flakes decided against it as they saw the snow piling up very quickly. Many out-of-town clients had planned to stay in the hotel, part of the Haywood Park complex, and did not need to leave the building, so there was little concern over lodging for them. I kept the audience up to date on the weather, but I was still in my usual "the threat is greatly exaggerated" mode and tried to calm fears of a paralyzing snowstorm.

By four o'clock, five inches of snow covered the ground, and there was no sign of it ending. My staff kept me apprised of rumors swirling about: the interstates were closing; several main traffic arteries were clogged with wrecks and cars unable to move in any direction. The auction was going well, though, and we still had a good crowd at five in the evening. But it was taking more effort for me to maintain my "don't worry about the snow" attitude.

There were about eighty people in the audience when I was told that the hotel restaurant had closed. I asked staff members to quickly call around to see what was still open. All downtown restaurants were either closed or about to close, their employees leaving for home. Even all McDonald's restaurants had called it a night. The problem soon became clear: Where would people eat?

I asked the crowd how many planned to spend the night; everyone raised their hands. The staff, perhaps tired of hearing that a beautiful snowstorm was a gift, smiled at me. I announced that food was going to be a bit of a problem, but we would work on it. I sent Fulton and Robin on a search mission to find available food for 100 people. We could have bought groceries at two stores that were still open, but we were hoping to find a better selection at a restaurant.

At seven that evening we moved chairs around and put together about a dozen folding tables, covered them with brown paper, and presented dinner for our faithful guests. A restaurant called Picnics was still open, and we had bought all the prepared food they had on hand. We were able to offer selections from two of the five major food groups, fried chicken and beer, with a few side dishes. It became a happy feast with many people sharing stories of past snowstorms and improvised solutions in emergencies.

It snowed all night, a steady, reassuring blanket of white. When I got up at five, I walked outside in the early morning stillness, the only sound the slight rustle of snow sifting through the bare trees.

I headed for downtown Asheville, hoping to piece together enough staff for the day's work, my headlights poking through layers of white, the flakes sliding past the windshield in long, smooth curves. With sustained effort, I was able to get to the Haywood Park Trade Mart, my tracks the only furrows through the twelve to sixteen inches of snow on most streets. When I got to the auction at about six, Fulton and Robin were already there; Fulton got around well with his four-wheel-drive truck and had picked up Robin on the way. No one has ever worked with two more loyal and resourceful people.

We had electricity and phone service, so the auction was on. The problem was getting staff to downtown Asheville. Fulton made several long runs to pick up people; some had stayed at my house and were relatively easy to pick up, but some were twelve or fifteen miles away. By nine o'clock we had a skeleton crew and were able to begin the auction. People wandered down from their rooms in the hotel, some yawning and stretching. Someone found a downtown restaurant open and serving coffee.

The auction moved at a slower pace than usual, only sixty lots an hour, but the prices were strong all day. Many people had a slightly festive "we survived the shipwreck" attitude, and paying well for a fine antique didn't seem like a big deal. Some said they wanted a souvenir of the snowstorm auction. Many stayed in Asheville for two or three days until they were comfortable driving on the roads.

For many years, people who had been our guests remembered the snowstorm with a smile and said they always hoped it would snow at another auction so we would buy them dinner again.

VIDEO

Mrs. Sondquist had called to ask if I would come to her home and look at her "things." She lived alone and was moving to assisted living. She said she had a house full of furniture, carpets, figurines, glassware, and linens, a lifetime accumulation she was not planning to take with her. She hoped something might be suitable for one of our auctions of fine antiques.

She lived in a large complex of condominiums just south of Asheville, one of many in the area designed for retirees. The names of these developments evoked halcyon English landscapes—Briar Cliff, Heather Ridge, Clear Brook—but I had never seen any cliffs, brooks, heather, or briars in these retirement communities. Their topography more often featured cul-de-sacs, eruptions of crape myrtle, and white plastic fences from Home Depot and Lowe's. I parked where Mrs. Sondquist had instructed, at the cracked asphalt curb with a stenciled yellow address: "3604 Visitor."

Planners and architects of these neighborhoods had created designs and structures that would circumscribe people's lives: roads, parking places, planted trees, flower beds, the arrangement of rooms. These patterns often gave rise to the fear that if I lived here, my life would enter a predictable, uneventful decline, planned by others. It smelled of confinement to me: the loss of choices, the expectation of conformity, the pulse of embedded routines. I was sixty-two years old and in good health the day of this visit in 2004; the strictures of life in such a place seemed far away.

Mrs. Sondquist met me at the front door, well-dressed for our appointment in a white blouse with a carved-shell cameo at the collar, a gray wool skirt, and large gold earrings. My khaki pants and blue shirt reflected expectations of a more modest occasion. "I really don't think there is anything here for you," she began. "I know you sell fine antiques, but I wanted you to look around and see the things in the basement," she continued, closing the door behind me. She was polite and composed, but her face, tight and unsmiling, suggested resignation, several fingers touching her lips as we spoke.

She led me into the living room and adjoining dining area, both orderly, brightly lit, and decorated without visible passion. On similar occasions, many clients would praise the beauty and value of their possessions, but Mrs. Sondquist expressed no enthusiasm as she pointed at upholstered furniture, Waterford vases, a shelf of books, and a reproduction tall case clock. She did not pick up anything to ask about its value or to confirm authenticity or provenance.

I shared her lack of excitement: her china a common Limoges pattern with pink apple blossoms, service for eight, but lacking three cups; her "paintings" were framed prints; her "silver" all silver plate, perhaps wedding gifts from the 1950s. The carpets, modern handwoven Persian rugs, had been expensive when purchased but now were worth only a fraction of the thousands originally paid. She moved quickly through the rooms, including the upstairs guest bedrooms, her hand waving across the modern beds, Victorian rockers, and brass-plated lamps. I reluctantly agreed with her; she had nothing suitable for our auctions.

We quickly ended up in the kitchen, where she pointed at the basement door and announced that we would now look at what was stored in the basement. We were working through her agenda. I had been there fifteen minutes.

The basement smelled of mold, and it housed scattered garden tools and packing crates. A treadmill spotted with mildew sat in a corner. One group of boxes with separating corrugations had faint "Xmas" markings, and a pair of folding wooden chairs, lacking seats, leaned against a wall. I saw only one small room that suggested order and use. The walls had exposed studs on the outside and shiny gray paneling in the interior, a color that collided with the orange carpet and the fluorescent lighting. Neatly arranged shelves lined all the walls.

The straight, clean rows of vertically boxed videocassettes were labeled in neat script: "New Zealand," "China," "Tuscany," "The Isle of Harris," "Belgium," "The Ukraine." There were dozens if not several hundred of them, most with accompanying maps, brochures, travel guides stacked alongside.

"Travel was our life," Mrs. Sondquist said quietly. I imagined photos of smiling middle-aged tourists in sunglasses, posing before stone walls, framed by pleasant churches or mountain peaks in the distance. Much of her adult life, now memories of itself, rested in this small, musty crypt.

"Mr. Brunk," she began, her face now anxious and deeply lined. This was the moment she had planned, the sentence she had rehearsed, the reason for my visit. "I am going to be moving, and I need help with this room." She explained that she had called the Center for Creative Retirement, the public library, several public schools, and program directors at three retirement centers to see if there would be any interest in her donation of their home-made videos and hundreds of photographs, with audio accompaniment arranged by her late husband, each illustrating their visit to a different region or country. For her, this would create an ongoing memorial of sorts to their life together: a way to continue it or to prolong its end. She explained, with a tone of surprise, that all the organizations she had contacted had politely declined her offer.

Did I know anyone who would be interested in this collection? Surely their travels would be of interest to someone. "The pictures are very sharp, and the background music for each video is by composers from the country we were visiting." She paused, as if to condense her sorrow into the fewest possible words. "I have no family," she said, her arms folded, fingers again pressed against her lips. The decline of her ability to travel and the loss of companionship had slowly closed in. The contents of these boxes, symbolic and tangible evidence that she and her husband had lived, were now the most difficult to part with.

She asked if she could call me when she got ready to move, "to take care of this for me." Instinctively, I said, "Yes, I will help," unable to imagine any other response to her grieving but not knowing what I could possibly do that she had not already done. Her voice rose in relief, and she finalized our arrangement by squeezing both my hands, her face now hopeful.

. . . .

Visits such as this sometimes triggered a confrontation with my own demise. I wondered what would be in my small room, the last place in which I would seek continuity in my life, when, due to age and frailty, I could no longer push back the shrinking edges of my world. Would it be boxes of perfectly shaped stones I had collected on the shingle beaches of Unst; or a folder of music, the pieces I had most enjoyed singing; or a collection of maps with thin green lines, marking places I had explored? Maybe in the end, it would be a box or two of family photos.

But why would I want to remember at all? Perhaps, as I neared the end of my life, I should close my eyes and enjoy the voids, the airy, quiet caverns now available to me. Maybe I could slide into death more cleanly if my small room was empty, if I no longer reached for the fragments of my life to which I could no longer connect. I imagined not having a small room at all, shutting my eyes and finally letting go of everything: all my possessions, all the relationships, sustaining and fractured, all the unfinished tasks, all the anxious worry over whether I had been truthful and kind, the urgent, the incomplete, the unexplained, and finally even the need to remember.

My work has often taken me to a closet or attic where I encountered a box of family photos. These pictures were presumed to be a resource for family members who might later want to know where they came from and what people and events had shaped their lives. As they sifted through these collections, I often heard an heir or descendant comment, "I have no idea who these people are." These accumulations are often passed along to the following generations, a picture or two occasionally retrieved and framed, its path to obscurity slowed for a generation or two—a hedge of sorts against certain namelessness.

. . . .

When my father died several years ago, I had experienced the complex tangle of feelings created by family photos. He had lived ninety-seven years. After his death, as my brother Stan and I sorted his remaining possessions, I agreed to inherit my father's 1,400 color slides, photos he had taken from the early 1930s to about 1970. He had left no instructions about the future of this collection. At family gatherings, he would often darken a room and "show his slides," and some became favorites: my mother wearing an odd hat and wrapped in a Navajo-style blanket; Stan and I as boys, waving from the windows of our black 1938 Ford.

Several months later, Stan came to visit, and for two long evenings, with the help of a large light box, we examined each color slide, looking for forgotten details. We sorted and condensed the collection into about 300 images: houses my father had lived in as a boy, family reunions, vacations, weddings, cute children, scenic views of mountains and oceans. Many photos pictured Stan and me, picking blackberries, playing in the snow, posing with our grandparents. We found very few spontaneous photos of individuals or groups; most were poses arranged by my father, who had told people where they should stand or sit and what to hold in their hand or point to.

Many of these pictures triggered familiar stories, bits of family lore, gossip, and semi-legends, Stan and I recalling who had done what. Identifying the people in the photos became a friendly contest. "You can tell that is Uncle Joe because his car's license plate is from California," Stan would say.

I had the 300 remaining slides reproduced on CDs, copies for Stan and me and others distributed to my father's five grandchildren, including my two adult children. This created the distinct possibility that one of those five grandchildren, or one of their thirteen children, would one day browse through those images and say, "I have no idea who those people are."

At one point, deep in a pile of similar photos of the same people, I asked Stan for whom we were doing this. He said, "Ourselves." I realized he was right; our time with the slides may have been their best moment. We had been the curators of my father's visual record of our family's history and folklore. We had created our own version of Mrs. Sondquist's basement archive.

She called about three months after my initial visit and introduced herself as the lady "with the room in the basement." I remembered her clearly and had hoped that she wouldn't call, that some change in circumstance had left her basement empty; perhaps one of the agencies had reconsidered and called her back to happily accept her offer. How foolish of me. "Could you come tomorrow morning?" she asked. She explained that the movers were almost finished, and the only thing left was the room in the basement. "It was so kind of you to offer to help," she added. I told her I would be there around nine the next morning. I wondered what she thought "help" really meant. It probably didn't matter; she no longer had to struggle with it. Mr. Brunk was dealing with it.

I quickly pictured possible ways I could donate her neatly labeled videos, even a few of them, to someone. Couldn't they be used as an enrichment series in an after-school program? Or in a survey course in world geography? Could someone use the audio portions in a music class?

I wondered if I should I look at a few videos myself or with my family, to pay at least minimal homage to this vast expenditure of time and energy. I imagined challenging, relentless boredom. How could anyone be interested in someone else's vacations: the hotel in which they stayed when they visited Copenhagen thirty years ago, the ship they took from Athens to Istanbul? Others whom she had contacted may have imagined a similar tedium, the minutiae of someone else's life.

Perhaps the videos could be combined into a continuous loop and be used in a work of conceptual art, an installation in which the photographs would be projected on the wall of a gallery in an unending cycle, the music playing in an unending cycle. Mrs. Sondquist's collection would then become a statement, an unforgiving satire of our modern, often transient preoccupation with visual images and the ever-present, concurrent layer of mindless noise in which we often live. The videos' ordinariness, their insular purpose, their lack of appeal, would now be their greatest attributes.

When I arrived in my Dodge van the next morning, Mrs. Sondquist met me at her front porch and led me to the basement door, which she had propped open. She explained that she had some final packing to do upstairs and slowly retreated up the carpeted steps. I packed all the videos into six large boxes and lugged them, one at a time, bulky and heavy, up the basement stairs. Then, using a hand truck, I moved them down the sidewalk, past several clumps of crape myrtle, and into the back of the van.

When I finished, I looked back toward the front door, where Mrs. Sondquist stood on the small concrete porch. From this distance, standing outside her now empty condominium, she looked especially old and frail. I wondered if her grief had shifted some, perhaps realigned, so she could feel the slight wave of relief offered by this moment. I walked back to her and asked if I could help with anything else. She replied that the people from assisted living would pick her up in a little while and that she had saved one chair to sit on while she waited.

I unloaded the boxes at our small office and warehouse on Carolina Lane and stacked them in the corner beside the big metal roll-up door but didn't label them. I stared at the pile and considered again that Mrs. Sondquist had "no family." I came from a large family with forty-four first cousins, and it is difficult for me to imagine fading to total obscurity, being known to no one. Surely some of my descendants will be able to recognize me in a photo, know my name, know that I had lived and perhaps remember that I built stone walls or made furniture. "I have no family" increases the chances that one will be utterly forgotten.

In 300 years, I may be the unknown tenth-generation ancestor of someone. Or does the Internet, and other not yet imagined conduits of information and memory, suggest that after death, we will all float in a semi-eternal state of being both remembered and forgotten?

About two years after stacking her boxes in our warehouse, I saw Mrs. Sondquist's obituary in the newspaper. She had lived in Cleveland, and her husband had grown up in Pennsylvania. He'd been an electrical engineer, and she had enjoyed volunteering in service clubs; theirs were seemingly unremarkable lives. The Sondquists had "traveled widely." No survivors were mentioned, but I had many survivors stored in my warehouse, all resting in dusty, sagging boxes.

I walked by them every day and occasionally considered their contents. Mrs. Sondquist's videos bore witness to the most essential elements of the life she had shared with her husband: their joy in exploring new cultures, their curiosity, their vitality, perhaps even their affection for each other. Perhaps that joy and affection was what she most wanted to preserve, not the boxes themselves. It lightened my concern about the boxes to think of them in this way. But other days, I felt as though I had become the guardian of her very life. In her own words, travel was Mrs. Sondquist's "life."

But even without the videos, she could arrange all her memories of their travels in her mind: sheep blocking a road in Scotland, a brilliant glacial lake in British Columbia, a smiling street vender in Kyoto. She was free to retrieve and hold these vestiges of their shared lives, hundreds, perhaps thousands, of them, and bring them into focus as she wished and perhaps smile at their remembrance. She could do this.

Death came to her with no regard for the videos or for any memories she may have carried in her heart. I wonder if in the writing of this account, I have satisfied Mrs. Sondquist's request that I take care of the room in her basement.

Occasionally, I hear of someone who apparently had no desire to be remembered, one who specified "no service," no gathering of friends and family to celebrate a life, no poems, no humorous anecdotes, no online registry, no granite obelisks, their ashes thrown to the wind. This would be the clean void of anonymity, an emptiness for which I am apparently unprepared. It is difficult for me to imagine not existing and to accept the absolute end of my life: finite, mortal, extinction. My life is all I have. I need to accept that, eventually, I will be forgotten.

I have instructed that my body be placed deep in the ground, unembalmed, wrapped only in a shroud. I am not so clear, though, about anonymity. Shouldn't there be a small marker somewhere, with my name and maybe a date, saying that I lived? I have, after all, put a lot of effort into my days. Something over 100 billion people have lived on this planet, however, and it is not clear to me why I would require a marker.

Recently, I read a summary of discoveries made by the powerful telescopes at the Swinburne University of Technology in Australia. They are able to detect 110,000 galaxies within 2 billion light-years of Earth; the most distant they have identified is over 13 billion light-years away. As the universe expands, this remote galaxy moves 800 miles farther away from our planet every second. It is estimated that only 1.6 percent of the entire universe will ever be observed from our planet. Mrs. Sondquist's life, her husband's life, my father's life, my brother's life, and my life will all have occupied immeasurably minuscule specks of time and space.

I was the only witness one still winter day as I carefully lowered Mrs. Sondquist's six heavy boxes into the dumpster outside the warehouse door.

ACKNOWLEDGMENTS

For the first ten years of my life as a writer, Jeremy Chamberlin, who teaches at the University of Michigan, was my editor; Chan Gordon of the Captain's Bookshelf in Asheville had introduced us. Many of the essays in this collection began as hesitant, wandering excursions, but under Jeremy's patient coaching, they grew into more substantial nonfiction prose. He gave me bibliographies of works to read and line edited much of my early work.

He also suggested I attend the Bear River Writers' Conference in northern Michigan, which I did every spring for seven years. The accomplished writers with whom I worked in that setting provided support and guidance, which continue to inform my writing: Richard Russo, Rhoda Janzen, Patricia Hampl, Jerry Dennis, Thomas Lynch, Keith Taylor, and Richard Tillinghast. After-hours poker games with several of these writers also provided memorable vocabulary.

On most Wednesday nights for the past ten years, I met with Dave Moore and George Peery, friends for over four decades and my first readers. In exchange for dinner, they provided candid and valuable commentary on my most recent work, including suggested revisions. They cheered me on when I despaired over how difficult it is to write well. Large quantities of Mexican, Thai, Korean, and Indian food and beverages have been consumed over discussions of the importance of interiority, the requirements of a stand-alone essay, the subtle joys of irony, and occasionally the premise of a *New Yorker* cartoon.

My gratitude also extends to the many people who assisted with research, editing, and proofreading or otherwise encouraged the existence of this book: Kent Shifferd, Elizabeth Kostova, Scott Carter, Bruce Johnson,

Lou Procter, Laura Crockett, Charlotte Wainwright, Peter Jaber, Deanne Levison, Dana Romeis, Judith Barkan, Faith Sandler, Bruce Kelly, Pat Fitzpatrick, Jim and Lynne Wilson, Dave Galentine, Gretchen Batra.

Special thanks go to Kathy Sheldon and Marcia Trahan for early editing of the manuscript.

Of the several hundred employees who have worked for Brunk Auctions, three in particular deserve my lasting gratitude: Robin Rice, Fulton Beville, and Jerry Israel. Without their steadfast commitment to the goals of the auction business and their collective ability to solve problems, the survival of the business might have been in doubt. In a similar fashion, members of the Brunk family have contributed a variety of suggestions, editing, and support: Ingrid, Jan, Andrew, Lauren, Stan, Barbara, Logan, Ellis, Stella, Silas, Eva, Emma, and Mable.

Cate Hodorowicz, my acquisitions editor at the University of North Carolina Press, told me when we first met that she would be my advocate throughout the lengthy process of creating this book. I am deeply grateful that she and all her colleagues have been that at every turn. Their suggestions, both large-scale and specific, have been invaluable.